BYRON
A Symposium

BYRON
A Symposium

edited by
JOHN D. JUMP

© John D. Jump 1975

All rights reserved. No part of this publication may be reproduced or transmitted, in any form or by any means, without permission.

First published 1975 by
THE MACMILLAN PRESS LTD
London and Basingstoke

Published in the U.S.A. 1975 by
HARPER & ROW PUBLISHERS, INC.
BARNES & NOBLE IMPORT DIVISION

ISBN: 0–06–493436–5

Photoset, printed and bound
in Great Britain

CONTENTS

	Preface	vii
	Notes on Contributors	xv
1	BYRON'S CORNISH ANCESTRY	1
	A. L. Rowse	
2	BYRON'S PROSE	16
	John D. Jump	
3	THE POET OF *CHILDE HAROLD*	35
	Francis Berry	
4	THE BYRONIC BYRON	52
	Gilbert Phelps	
5	BYRON AND THE SATIRIC TEMPER	76
	P. M. Yarker	
6	THE STYLE OF *DON JUAN* AND AUGUSTAN POETRY	94
	A. B. England	
7	DON JUAN IN SEARCH OF FREEDOM: BYRON'S EMERGENCE AS A SATIRIST	113
	W. Ruddick	
8	'A LIGHT TO LESSON AGES': BYRON'S POLITICAL PLAYS	138
	Anne Barton	
9	ROMANCE IN BYRON'S *THE ISLAND*	163
	P. D. Fleck	
	Index	185

PREFACE

Most of the essays in this collection derive from lectures given in London, Cambridge, and Manchester in commemoration of the 150th anniversary of Byron's death; all of them have been written with that commemoration in mind. Eight of the contributors seek to define the special insights and pleasures to be obtained from reading what Byron wrote. The other sheds an oblique light on the poet's life and character.

Readers used often to complain that they could find very little interesting discussion of Byron's literary achievement. There was any amount of writing about him, but it was overwhelmingly concerned with the man rather than with his work. The complaint was valid until around fifteen years ago. Then, shortly before and after 1960 a number of unusually important biographical studies appeared. These must temporarily have sated the curiosity they were designed to satisfy, for between then and the sesquicentenary the literary critics had the field largely to themselves. Each of them was liable to congratulate himself on being a lonely pioneer, but in fact the 1960s and the earlier 1970s saw the publication of a great deal of literary criticism of Byron's poetry. In most of this the poems in the octave stanza received the highest praise, in conformity with a well-established trend in British and American criticism. But there appeared also scholarly and perceptive studies of Byron's work in other forms, including that written during his earlier years.

The fact that 1974 witnessed a considerable resumption of biographical activity should surprise no one. Centenaries of authors commonly have that effect, and the present volume opens appropriately with an essay in which a Cornishman describes some of Byron's Cornish relatives. A. L. Rowse concentrates mainly upon Sophia Trevanion, who was Byron's paternal grandmother, and Henry Trevanion, who was the great-grandson of Sophia's sister. Having married one daughter of Augusta Leigh, Henry became the lover of another, Medora, who is commonly believed to have been Byron's child by Augusta, his half-sister. Medora's relationship with Trevanion evidently ruined a great part of her short life. Sophia, the poet's ancestor and Medora's, seems to have been an intelligent and attractive woman. Her husband was 'Foulweather Jack', the admiral whom the poet mentions more than once in his writings. From her and from his mother, Rowse claims, Byron inherited 'the Celtic temperament'.

Generalisations about racial characteristics are notoriously tricky, but this phrase can serve us by drawing attention to Byron's remarkable mobility of thought and feeling. Thanks to this, his letters and journals exhibit a simply astonishing versatility. Reviewing the new edition of these that began to appear in 1973, Michael Foot, himself an able literary man as well as a successful politician, suggested that Byron was the finest letter-writer in the English language. The second essay in the present collection is designed to support some such assessment.

Its essential plea is that Byron's journals and letters should be read not only as informative documents but also as, in effect, dramatic monologues. They reveal and characterise their author as he writes; they record responses to his immediate situation that compel us to realise it in our turn; and his distinctive tone with each correspondent brings that correspondent vividly before our imagination. Utterly informal prose in intention, Byron's letters and journals do at their frequent best achieve the status of works of art.

From an early age he exhibits in them his wit and humour, his gaiety and playfulness, his shrewd observation of men and manners, and his sardonic realism. But these are attributes that it will take him years to introduce effectively in his verse. Even so, his early poetry, though deprived of so much that might have enriched it, embraces many powerful and deeply impressive achievements. Francis Berry celebrates the chief of these in his lecture on *Childe Harold's Pilgrimage*.

The subject calls for eloquence, and Berry supplies it. He writes as a member of the literary generation that grew up in Britain and America during the period of T. S. Eliot's predominance as poet and critic. Those who followed Eliot in prizing above all a poetry that was complex and diffident were naturally prone to dismiss Byron's as commonplace and crude. But today we no longer esteem hesitancy and scepticism so highly. Social and political passions have regained urgency among us, even to the extent of manifesting themselves in deplorable acts of destruction. In the world as it now is, claims Berry, a poetry of drive, vigour, and assurance, a poetry that celebrates heroes and action, a rhetorical poetry, has become very much to the point.

No one is likely to accept this view without question. Perhaps Berry has drawn too sharp a contrast between the 1930s and the 1970s. But the contrast as he draws it is admirably dramatic, and it enables him to praise *Childe Harold's Pilgrimage* for qualities such as Byron's contemporaries found in it, and at the same time to see these qualities as relevant to our modern situation. Defenders of *Childe Harold's Pilgrimage* have occasionally tried to detect in it the virtues proper to the Age of Eliot. Berry's lecture convinces us, if we needed convincing, that they were simply asking the wrong questions. The young Byron with whom he leaves us is a political liberal and 'a man speaking to men'. He has a sharp sense of fact and a proper appreciation of the enduring importance of great historical events. He uses words skilfully to sway a large and important audience.

This audience rapidly became international. In country after country, readers and writers surrendered to the Byronic spell. The French proved particularly susceptible. They had felt the heady idealism of the early years of their Revolution, and they had felt the sour disillusionment of the aftermath, down to the Restoration of the despised Bourbons in 1815. The Byronic hero, a man embittered by the virtual extinction of a hope which nevertheless struggles to survive, might have been made for them. *The Giaour* astonished Alfred de Vigny and dazzled Lamartine; Lamartine thought *Childe Harold's Pilgrimage* the only epic possible in his day. Hugo, de Musset, Gautier, and George Sand also responded to the Byronic influence. It reached Goethe and Heine in Germany, Leopardi in Italy. It spread even to Russia. In order to read the English poet in the original, Pushkin studied his language; he alludes to him repeatedly in *Eugene Onegin*; and he sometimes employs a truly Byronic irony at his expense:

> By a most happy whim Lord Byron
> Has clothed a hopeless egoism
> In saturnine romanticism.
> (III.xii)

Lermontov in *A Hero of Our Own Times* portrays a very fully developed Byronic hero. Early experience, a sceptical habit of mind, and an excessive self-consciousness have made Pechorin cold, egotistical, and destructive.

> My mind has been corrupted by the world, my fancy is fickle, my heart insatiable, everything seems petty; I get used to sorrow as quickly as to enjoyment, and my life grows emptier day by day. One expedient is still left me—travel.
> ('Bela')

Both the predicament and the solution are those Byron confers on Childe Harold at the beginning of his pilgrimage.

The Byron who exercised this wide sway was not the comic and satirical poet of the octave stanza, the author of *Beppo*, *Don Juan*, and *The Vision of Judgment*, but what Gilbert Phelps calls 'the Byronic Byron', the author of *Childe Harold's Pilgrimage*, the Turkish tales, and *Manfred*. Phelps stresses the difficulty of the Byronic Byron's problem. Genuinely feeling an impatience with his 'sedentary trade' such as Yeats later professed to feel, he sought to reconcile Romantic aspirations with the unalterable facts of the contemporary situation and of the human condition in general. He could not for this purpose employ either the established techniques of eighteenth-century poetry or the newer techniques which his Romantic contemporaries were developing. His solution was bold and original: he gave the freest possible scope to his creative energy and wrote a swiftly-moving rhetorical poetry that simply asks to be read in long stretches.

During the middle years of the twentieth century, shortbreathed devotees of 'close analysis' used to deplore its lack of conciseness and concentration. But they are no longer in a position to impose their preferences on the rest of us; and those with the mental stamina to enjoy Byron's long, symphonic movements may easily shrug off their scolding.

Phelps has much more to say than this. He rightly emphasises, for example, the importance in the Byronic Byron of the notion of a lost innocence which experience has rendered irretrievable and which remains a tantalising memory. He shows that the Byronic hero is an embodiment both of the spirit of revolt and of the sense of blighted hopes. Above all, he argues that such extended and recurrent images as the Byronic hero, whatever fault we may find with particular presentations, acquire a bold impressiveness from the furious energy which creates and sustains them.

This brings back to mind the drive, vigour, and assurance praised by Berry. Both critics, in fact, are indicating the quality which more than any other gave Byron his vast nineteenth-century reputation throughout Europe and beyond it. To a greater extent than Berry, Phelps dwells upon the profound pessimism which accompanied Byron's defiant liberalism. Much that he claims for the Byronic Byron could be said with equal truth of the comic and satirical Byron. But there is no need to defend *Don Juan* against him. He is ready to agree that it is Byron's masterpiece.

In the three essays that follow, Patrick Yarker, A. B. England, and W. Ruddick take this for granted and ask questions relating to Byron's development as a satirical poet. Within the broad limits of their consensus, they develop some interesting divergences of view.

Yarker writes on the early satires, in which, he says, Byron models himself on Pope and Gifford but lacks the seriousness and purposefulness of his masters. For complete success in the genre, Byron has to discover a form in which he can express his satirical sense of the gap between the actual and the ideal – the gap which Phelps sees the Byronic Byron as striving to close – with the cheerful ease his friends and correspondents already recognised in him. He finds this form in J. H. Frere's 'Whistlecraft' poem, and he achieves his complete success in *Beppo*.

Some of Yarker's insights should interest the critic who will one day explore carefully the literary relationship of Byron and Gifford. This was, after all, a very odd relationship indeed. In 1812, when the two men entered into communication, Byron was a youthful Whig poet of aristocratic birth, Gifford a middle-aged Tory scholar and critic of plebeian origin. Yet Byron revered Gifford, not merely as the satirist responsible for *The Baviad* and *The Maeviad* but in all his roles as a man of letters. For years he was to allow the admired and admiring Gifford to choose for him, and in his absence, between alternative readings that he would leave in the manuscripts of his poems. A creative writer could hardly have shown a more entire trust.

Without denying that Byron often writes in the Augustan tradition represented by Pope, England argues that the style of *Don Juan* connects even more significantly with that of Swift. Perceptive close analyses of specimen passages from all three poets enable him to claim that, whereas Pope in describing a chaotic miscellaneousness will invariably evoke the principle of order which the confusion flouts, Swift and Byron are alike in more commonly doing nothing of the sort but allowing the chaotic miscellaneousness to stand as their offered vision of reality. *Don Juan* is extremely varied, of course; the early part of Canto XIV is not the only place where Byron is certainly writing as a successor to Pope; but the literary affiliation that England traces keeps us in mind of the negative and destructive aspects of what remains at the same time a paradoxically cheerful poem.

In Ruddick's view, Byron was inhibited in his early work by his observance of the Augustan distinctions between genres and between styles. To be sure, he achieved some powerful successes within these limits. But for the full fruition of his particular gifts he had to transcend the distinctions he had inherited. Ruddick holds that his friend Thomas Moore, the Irish lyrist, helped him to do this. Moore was already developing in *The Twopenny Post-Bag* 'a light, urbane, rapid-paced, and aristocratically toned satire of a kind which was genuinely new'. Byron learned from him as well as from Frere, and in the resultant *ottava rima* poems he revitalised Popean satire for his own very different age. This is the case above all in *The Vision of Judgment* and in the late cantos of *Don Juan* which bring its hero to England. These late cantos point straight forward to the Victorian novel.

During the years which we now tend to imagine as dominated by the composition of *Don Juan*, Byron wrote also a number of plays. Undeterred by his insistence that he wrote them only for the reading public, Anne Barton urges the staging of *Marino Faliero*, *The Two Foscari*, and *Sardanapalus*. She believes that this would lead to a correct appreciation of them as finely reasoned political tragedies. Like other contributors to the present volume, she is constantly impressed by the relevance today of what Byron wrote in that earlier age of revolutions. She finds it possible to compare him as a playwright with Brecht, who likewise aimed through historical dramas to change men's minds and influence their actions. Both of them wished to make their audiences think and declined to facilitate mere escape 'into a world of daydreams and somnambulist repose'.

There follows a further attempt to secure a more favourable reception for comparatively neglected work. P. D. Fleck praises Byron's last complete poem, *The Island*, as at once unmistakably Romantic and unmistakably Byronic. In his view, it affirms the possibility of bringing the world of our heart's desire into alignment with the world we have in any case to accept as given. *The Island* briefly closes that gap between the ideal and the real which Phelps describes the Byronic Byron as striving to close. An inescapable awareness of this same gap is what Yarker, as we have seen, thinks fundamental to the satire of Byron and others.

Of the contributors to the present collection, some seek to justify further the current high estimate of certain of Byron's works, while others seek to promote more favourable responses to works they think still underrated. I have welcomed a similar variety in approach and in presentation. Some of the papers keep fairly closely to the lecture form; others have been written, or rewritten, as articles for reading. I have been happy to see each study take the particular form that was best suited for it and have left each author to judge for himself how extensive an apparatus of references his own contribution required, and to some extent what form these references might most appropriately take. But, in view of the fact that L. A. Marchand's edition of the letters and journals began in 1973 to supersede R. E. Prothero's, I have ensured that all exact references to this material take the form merely of the dates of the letters or diary-entries in question. These dates will suffice to enable readers to trace quotations in whichever text is the more readily accessible to them.

The British Council, the Byron Society, and the Extra-Mural Departments of the Universities of London and Manchester sponsored the lectures out of which most of the following papers developed. My last words here must be an expression of gratitude to them.

Manchester John D. Jump

NOTES ON CONTRIBUTORS

ANNE BARTON has recently relinquished the Carlile Chair of English at Bedford College, London, and has become Fellow and Tutor in English Literature at New College, Oxford, and University Lecturer in English. As Anne Righter she published *Shakespeare and the Idea of the Play* (1964). She is now married to John Barton of the Royal Shakespeare Company. Her present paper is a companion piece to her Nottingham Byron Foundation Lecture (1968).

FRANCIS BERRY, Professor of English, Royal Holloway College, London, is author of *The Galloping Centaur*, *Morant Bay and Other Poems*, and *Ghosts of Greenland* (verse); and of *Poets' Grammar, Poetry and the Physical Voice*, *The Shakesperian Inset*, and *Thoughts on Poetic Time* (criticism).

A. B. ENGLAND teaches at the University of Victoria, British Columbia. He is the author of a forthcoming book, *Byron's 'Don Juan' and Eighteenth-Century Literature*, and is at present engaged in a study of Swift's poetry.

P. D. FLECK, Professor of English, University of Western Ontario, London, Canada, has lectured widely on Byron and Shelley and is currently working on a study of the influence of these poets on each other. The essay published in the present volume was first prepared as the Byron Memorial Lecture, given at the Royal Institution, London, for the Byron Society, 17 April 1974.

JOHN D. JUMP, Professor of English, University of Manchester, has published critical studies of and editions of works by various Renaissance playwrights, Byron, Tennyson, and Matthew Arnold. He is general editor of the Critical Idiom series. His *Byron* appeared in 1972.

GILBERT PHELPS has worked in higher education and for the B.B.C.; he is now a freelance writer, lecturer, and broadcaster. The latest of several books on Latin America, *The Tragedy of Paraguay*, and his ninth novel, *The Low Roads*, are due in 1975. He has published an anthology, *The Byronic Byron* (1971), has written programmes on the poet for the B.B.C., and is continuing to work on him.

A. L. ROWSE, historian and poet, leading authority on the Age of Shakespeare, is first and last a Cornishman. Everything Cornish, at home and abroad, interests him. In his essay published in the present volume, he brings to light new information about Byron's Cornish ancestry and relations, which has its importance for understanding the poet's background and temperament.

W. RUDDICK teaches at the University of Manchester. He has written on Byron's historical tragedies and on Byron's relations with Thomas Moore. He is currently engaged on a study of the poetry of George Crabbe.

P. M. YARKER teaches at King's College, London. The nineteenth century is his area of special interest, and he has published editions of works by Wordsworth and Ruskin.

1 BYRON'S CORNISH ANCESTRY*

A. L. Rowse

Many people will know beautiful and romantically situated Caerhays Castle in Cornwall, not far from St Austell, its Nash tower and turrets rising above that lovely valley to look down on the beach below. A very appropriate setting for the poet's Cornish ancestry, though not many people know about that side to him. The Castle was built by his Trevanion cousins, who practically bankrupted themselves in doing so and sold it to the Williams family, who created there the finest garden in Cornwall.

Byron's genius was the product of several odd strains, not only the Byron. On his mother's side, a Gordon, he was a Highland Celt; but on his father's side he was a Cornish Celt, for the mother of 'Mad Jack' Byron was Sophia Trevanion of Caerhays. Really, Byron had no chance of achieving the equable, easy-going temper of an Englishman – Shakespeare, for example; Byron had all the disadvantages – and advantages – of the Celtic temperament.

When he was anxious to take his seat in the House of Lords, he was held up for some time for want of the marriage certificate of his grandparents. A messenger had to be sent down to Cornwall for affidavits proving the marriage, for Sophia Trevanion and her sailor-husband had been married not in a parish church but in a private chapel at Caerhays, in August 1748.

The Trevanions were a fascinating family of old indigenous Cornish gentry, like the Trevelyans, reaching right back to the Middle Ages. They were good fighting stock, going to sea or producing vice-admirals and sheriffs of Cornwall, with an heroic figure who died fighting for Charles I in the Civil War, one of 'the four wheels of Charles's wain'.

In mid-eighteenth century the male line at Caerhays failed –

* This chapter originally appeared as two articles in *The Times*.

though there are still plenty of Trevanions about today (one of them the Grand Bard of Cornwall) – and the estate fell to two coheiresses. The elder married a Bettesworth and got Caerhays, where they remained for a couple more generations and took back the old name.

Young Byron was well aware of his Bettesworth–Trevanion cousins, as they were of him. We find him writing from Trinity College, Cambridge, in October, 1807:

> I am going to sea for four or five months with my cousin, Captain Bettesworth, who commands the *Tartar*. We are going probably to the West Indies, or to the Devil; if there is a possibility of taking me to the latter, Bettesworth will do it. For he has received four-and-twenty wounds in different places, and at this moment possesses a letter from the late Lord Nelson stating Bettesworth as the only officer of the Navy who had more wounds than himself.

Young Byron did not go with his cousin, for in a matter of months Bettesworth was killed off Bergen. We see something of what the male stock was like; what about the female?

Sophia Trevanion was no less spirited and courageous – she had a difficult life with her admiral-husband and temperamental family; she was vivacious, with all the ups and downs of a Celtic nature, good-hearted or, rather, what the Cornish call 'feeling-hearted'. Dr Johnson described her, not pejoratively, as a *feeler;* he also said gallantly, 'she has the courage becoming an Admiral's Lady'.

In addition to this, she was highly intelligent, one of the bluestockings – surely this intellectual strain is important in the make-up of a writer like Byron, where the rest of his family were so given to action? Sophia was a great friend of the portentous Mrs Montagu, dear Fanny Boscawen, the piquante Mrs Thrale, clever Miss Burney and Dr Johnson. To have been approved of by Dr Johnson was something indeed; though of the various ladies who made attempts on his heart, he could not recall that Sophia had tried – 'perhaps her voice is low', and the Doctor we know was deaf.

She had her work cut out with her sailor-husband and needed all her Trevanion spirit to support it. In the first place, it was no sinecure being married to him — he gave her three sons and seven daughters. In the second place, he was very unfaithful. In 1773 a story was published about his escapades — something in the line of Fanny Hill: he was recognisable as the 'Nautical Lover' found discovered in bed with his chambermaid, whom the wife dismissed. He thereupon found lodgings for her in London; his wife pursued, and followed him to her retreat. He was fain to set the girl up in more secluded quarters, who was so devoted to him that 'she rejected considerable sums of money for temporary gratifications, and even settlements.' Mrs Thrale, who was nothing if not arch, used to describe Sophia as married to the Admiral 'pour ses péchés.'

We cannot go into his nautical career here; but we may well wonder whether it was not from Plymouth that Sophia chased her errant spouse, for he was in command of the guardship there in 1753–6, and it was there at Plymouth in 1756 that the poet's father was born.

The admiral was a well known figure in his day, as 'Foulweather Jack', from the appalling experiences he had endured when shipwrecked on the coast of Patagonia when young. In the vivid ship-wreck scene in *Don Juan* the poet made use of these from 'my grand-dad's Narrative'.

We must confine ourselves here to grandmother and the Trevanion stock. Here we are at once struck by how inter-mixed they all are, several of them marrying cousins, so that the Trevanion strain is doubled, though people have not noticed it, for it runs in the female line concealing the name. Sophia Trevanion, in marrying John Byron, was already marrying a first cousin (of the two daughters of Lord Berkeley of Stratton, in Cornwall, one married John Byron's father, the other Sophia's father). In the next generation William, heir to the 'Wicked' Lord Byron, eloped with his cousin Juliana, who was Sophia's daughter.

In the third generation the poet Byron was in love with his halfsister, Augusta, as we all know; what is not generally known that

Augusta's husband, Colonel Leigh, was their first cousin too; they were all three Sophia's grand-children. So that in their children the Trevanion strain was doubled.

It is generally recognised that Medora Leigh was Byron's child by Augusta, who proceeded to marry her eldest daughter Georgiana to her cousin, Henry Trevanion of the Caerhays family. But he fell in love with her sister, Medora, and – though of pious Evangelical persuasions and author of a volume of poems, *The Influence of Apathy* – seduced her, lived with her for some years and gave her three children. They had a passionate fixation on each other, and were horribly fertile.

There is a great deal more information about the Trevanions, of which I am the repository; all we need say here is that this background makes more clear Byron's obsession with the now fashionable incest-theme prominent in several of his works. I do not profess to understand the attraction – evidently something to do with chromosomes, as in the historic Ravallet case in France in the reign of Henri IV.

All this in her numerous descendants carrying on the *égaré* Trevanion strain must have been remote enough from good Sophia's mind – no one ever said an ill word against her. Indeed in Mrs Thrale's rating of her bluestocking friends, Sophia came second only to the impeccable Mrs Montagu and beat even her for good humour and useful knowledge. Even Fanny Boscawen, another admiral's wife – whom I adore – came third to Sophia's second. But Sophia was always elegant and animated; Mrs Thrale speaks of her 'warmth and brilliancy' and decides that she *loved* Sophia best, though she *liked* Mrs Montagu and Miss Burney best.

Sophia was sharp and perceptive too. Of one of the bluestocking ladies who sparkled, but remained unmarried, Sophia said, 'she is everybody's admiration, and nobody's choice'. Mrs Byron noticed Piozzi's infatuation for Mrs Thrale long before such a thought entered that artless head. Piozzi was singing 'Rassereno il tuo bel Ciglio' etc *at* Hester Thrale, when Sophia said, 'I suppose you *know* that man is in love with you'.

The idea of Mrs Thrale marrying *that man*, a mere singer, and an Italian too, divided their society from top to bottom and broke Dr

Johnson's heart. But Sophia remained loyal, when the errant couple returned from Italy, to be cut by all 'the old bluestocking society'. Piozzi, who was a charming man, made up to Mrs Byron like anything and in the end conquered any prejudice she had against him on the score of class.

Sophia's experience with her sailor-husband had inured her to the facts of life, and once she shocked pious Mrs Thrale by lending her an obscene poem – 'concerning the geranium flower; 'tis not very long, and 'tis I think exceedingly ingenious, but so obscene I will not pollute my book with it . . . though strongly tempted to copy or get it by heart'. What a pity! For Hester thought it 'mighty clever in its way, *that it is*'.

But now, September 1779, in the third year of the American Revolutionary war, Mrs Byron was in great trouble over her husband. He had been sent in command of a squadron to follow D'Estaing to the West Indies, who had a more powerful fleet and captured Grenada. In such a small society rumours flew about and, in those days, people took these disgraces very much to heart. (Admiral Byng had been shot, as Voltaire said, *pour encourager les autres*.) A friend of Mrs Thrale had scampered off with a cornet of horse; 'Mrs Byron, another flighty friend whom I love better than she deserves, is distressed just now. Her husband is supposed to have forborne fighting in this last affair, the loss of the Grenada Islands. And she is wild with grief.'

The tender heart of the great bear, Dr Johnson, is touched:

> Poor Mrs Byron! I am glad that she runs to you at last for shelter – give her, dear madam, what comfort you can. Her husband, so much as I hear, is well enough spoken of, nor is it supposed that he had power to do more than has been done.

Soon came word that it was a false alarm: Admiral Barrington arrived, and 'gives Byron the best of characters'.

Then there were her children to worry her. We all know what a scapegrace the poet's handsome father, 'Mad Jack', was; now her respectable younger son has brought a wife back from Barbados whom he hadn't known till ten days before he left. Miss Burney comments:

> a pleasant circumstance for this proud family! Poor Mrs Byron seems destined for mortification and humiliation; yet such is her *native fire* that, though half mad one day with sorrow and vexation, she is fit the next to entertain an assembly of company, and make them all happy.

Again, 'Her charming spirits never fail her . . . she bears up against all calamity.'

As well as the sons there were the daughters to worry the old lady. Sophia, 'having an independent fortune, has quarrelled with her mother and lives with one of her sisters, Mrs Byron, who married a first cousin, son of Lord Byron'. If he had lived, he would have succeeded to the title, not the poet; on his death, his widow married again and became Lady Wilmot.

In 1789, the year of the *revanche* the French suffered for their intervention in the American War, Mrs Thrale is writing that Mrs Byron's 'style of prettiness was such that men would willingly run through fire'; now, though old, she 'yet retains that elegance of form and manner' – she was like a decayed beauty in whom the lady of quality still appeared, though subdued. Now she is cast down by Lady Wilmot's death: 'not a daughter goes near her and the only son that should be her comfort is now in India'. His son, Sophia's grandson, succeeded the poet as seventh Lord Byron.

When the admiral died in 1786 he left his widow an estate of £1600 a year – most of which had come from Sophia's inheritance (some £12,000). Lady Wilmot was left £2000, but only £500 to the poet's father, 'that scapegrace Jack, who has behaved in a most shocking manner to his Mother and goes on as usual like a Rascal.' Within five years, having run through everything of his two wives, he was dead in France (1791).

His mother had died the previous year down at Bath, where she was living at the Belvedere. From her death-bed, at her last gasp, she wrote an affectionate farewell to Mrs Piozzi (who considered that she had helped forward her salvation). She was buried in the Abbey Church, 12 November 1790. Mrs Piozzi in her Journals gave her a character for 'Nobleness, elegance, animated beauty – promptitude of wit, capacity for thought', and considered putting up a little tablet to her memory, since none of her family bestirred himself to do so. (Her son put up one to his Barbados wife.) Nor did Hester put up anything in the end; however, it gave her an excuse to compose an epitaph, which contains some descriptive lines:

> . . . no more her high Descent we trace
> In each fine feature of the' expressive face;
> While polished ease with sprightliness combined
> In every sentence spoke the vigorous mind.

Such was Byron's Cornish grandmother, a personality to remember.

* * *

One day some years ago, in the dining-room of an hotel along the Great North Road, I looked up to see the self-same Medusa-like head that had looked down upon the fatal honeymoon of Byron and of Annabella Milbanke that snowy New Year 1815. There it was, blank and uncomprehending, in the decorative cornice that had been removed from her home, Halnaby Hall just up the road. It gave one a strange thrill to realise what it was and to think of the train of events that marriage set off: they did not seem so far away.

Everything about Byron is touched with strangeness – one of the sources of the irresistible attraction people found in him, and still find today. His was a radioactive personality that had shattering effects on all who came in contact with him. One sees it at work in the next generation as well as in his own.

There were no fewer than four Byron–Trevanion marriages; they seemed bent on marrying cousins and this doubled the Trevanion strain, somewhat lost to view through being on the female side, though no less strong for that. We know what a fixation Byron had on his half-sister and everyone considered that her third daughter, Medora – named after a character in *The Corsair,* a tale he was writing at the time – was his.

We can now observe the same obsessive fixation working itself out in the next generation, in the passion Medora and her cousin Henry Trevanion had for each other. Catherine Turney tells the story, from the English and French sources, in her book, *Byron's Daughter* (London, 1974). There remain the Cornish sources. She is very sympathetic to Medora, wholly unsympathetic to Trevanion – perhaps understandably; all the same, he has to be considered and the passion was mutual.

The awkward thing was that Henry had been married off to Medora's eldest sister, Georgiana. This was Augusta's doing – 'dearest Moe' as he wrote to her: she had more than a soft spot for the young man and may well have seduced him. She always defended him in the complications that ensued; Colonel Leigh detested Henry – he disapproved and was jealous.

Since Augusta was a lady-in-waiting to Queen Charlotte, with apartments in St James's Palace, the wedding took place in the Royal chapel on 4 February 1826. It was not two years since Byron's death. Nobody in either family attended, except Augusta and Medora. There was no money as usual and, as usual in the family, Lady Byron was called on to provide the wherewithal. She lent the young couple a house she had leased near Canterbury; Augusta, like the 'goose' she was – by which endearment Byron had called her – sent Medora along for company.

Georgiana – Georgey as she was known – was soon pregnant. Unfortunately she had little interest for Henry, though he gave her three daughters. Georgey seems to have been dull, and rather afraid of being left alone with Henry; they could not get on and both were glad of Medora's company as a safety-valve. To Henry she was more: with her Byron-dark hair and sexual temperament, at fifteen, he found her all too attractive.

Henry Trevanion had intellectual pretensions, as we see from the volume of verse he produced next year, *The Influence of Apathy, and other Poems,* published by Longman in 1827. Nobody seems to have read it for the light it throws on him. It happens that I possess Georgey's own copy, with her name written thus in it.

Three years before Henry had been the only member of the family, along with the Colonel, to attend the melancholy funeral procession of his cousin to the vault at Hucknall Torkard. The little volume reflects something of the mighty shadow cast by the dead poet, though on the eighteenth-century moralising side of his work: this, together with the 'sensibility' which Jane Austen made fun of in her novel contemporaneously, made up Trevanion's poetic personality.

A prose argument prefaces the work.

> The disposition of youth to engage unadvisedly in friendships. The inefficacy of public or private tuition to avert the evils . . . to invalidate the temptations of sin. The tendency of a career of sin to deaden the sensibility of our affections.

He deplored

> too frequent contemplation of reverses sustained by the virtuous and the triumphs of the vicious. The consequently increased influence of temptation and the miseries from yielding to it. The probability that repeated afflictions will annihilate the kindly sympathies of our nature. The passion excited by trifling annoyance; fatal consequence of yielding to it, as operating on the heart: exception, BYRON. Tranquillity of mind attainable only by the means of apathy.

Such was the moral, enforced in rhymed couplets:

> Oh! woman! jewelled link of being's chain,
> First dream of love, last object of disdain,
> Sad is the storm, o'erwhelming is the sea,
> Star of the soul! that turns our course from thee:
> But all must be forgotten, all must cease
> But Apathy, for him who seeks on earth for peace.

Attached to the poem is a series of references as pretentious as that the young Eliot attached to *The Waste Land.* Not only are Herodotus and Plutarch cited, there are esoteric quotations from Popilius Laenas (who ever he was), Papirius, St Sopistratus; Gibbon,

Locke and to show how up-to-date he was Trevanion's fellow-Celt, Chateaubriand.

The second section consists of personal poems on love and friendship, one to L.E.L., the notorious poetess whom he knew: these are pale imitations of Byron, with a tribute:

> Childe Harold ceased to strike the lyre—
> Upon his grave untuned it lay—
> And nations came there to admire,
> But mortal hand would not aspire
> Upon the strings to play.

Several poems refer to calm summer seas, or the 'little barks gliding over the slumbering wave'. One thinks of the old house at Caerhays, just then being transformed into a romantic castle by Nash, looking down upon the cove and the open sea beyond.

One poem is addressed 'To J. T——n, Esq, On his Singing'. This is evidently Henry's elder brother, John, the heir to Caerhays, whom Byron knew. In April 1808 Byron was writing, 'I have been introduced to Julia Byron by Trevanion at the Opera; but I do not admire her, there is too much Byron in her countenance'. Another grand-daughter of Sophia, she was too clever, which Byron considered 'a very great defect in a woman, who becomes conceited in course'. Shades of poor Annabella and the fatal marriage to come!

For all Henry's praise of apathy, he was anything but apathetic in bed. Georgey was not only pregnant (again), but so was Medora and the neighbours at Canterbury were beginning to talk. Lady Byron was not without her intelligence system; Augusta had neither intelligence nor an intelligence system and 'did not appear to have a suspicion of any kind'. The youthful *ménage* popped across the Channel, where Medora gave birth to a boy – to Henry's further grievance against poor Georgey who gave him only daughters. The child was put out to nurse and shortly died. All three trooped back to England, without a penny to bless them.

Medora, now sixteen, took refuge with 'dearest Moe' at St James's Palace, where 'Mr Trevanion came very often, almost daily, to visit me, and his visits were not in any way discouraged by my mother'. They spent a good deal of time reading the Bible together, for Augusta delighted in giving Bibles to everybody – she had given Byron one, which he took everywhere with him on his travels. Besides, Henry was rather religious.

At New Year 1831 Medora discovered that she was 'likely to become a mother' again – she was not yet seventeen. Henry took laudanum before disclosing 'the fatal cause of my misery'. All Augusta's sympathies were with poor Henry: 'you know how I have loved and regarded you as my own Child – I can never cease to do so', etc. For her own erring child there were only religious reproaches:

> you know that I confidently hoped and intended you to be confirmed this Easter. I suppose it is now hopeless – consult your own heart and wishes. I hoped to be able to prepare you sufficiently myself with the help of reading – but now I feel it would be a great satisfaction to me if some Clergyman were to assist in this.

Augusta's easy-going nature had opened the way to all this – it had been one of her chief charms in Byron's eyes, that and the fact that she didn't argue; but their daughter couldn't have a baby in St James's Palace. Henry and his wife were taking a house outside Bath, quarrelling more than ever; Georgey needed Medora as a buffer, Henry needed her as something more. The deleterious trio all were installed together, when Colonel Leigh descended on them and carried the erring Medora off to a hide-out near Regent's Park, where pregnant girls of good family could have their babies behind locked doors and barred windows. This time Medora had a stillborn child.

Henry was not giving her up: he planned to abscond with her to France, leaving Georgey behind.

They lived together in France for several years, under the name of Monsieur and Madame Aubin. Henry would have got a divorce if he could; since that proved impossible, Medora joined the Catholic Church. We gather that 'Henry was sexually obsessed by her and that she responded with equal passion'. There were frequent miscarriages; Henry was very keen to have a healthy living child by her. They opted to settle by the little town of Carhaix in Brittany – oddly enough: was Henry drawn by the name? For it was the same as Carhays, or Caerhays, in Cornwall whence his family had drawn their sustenance for some 500 years.

The finances of his family were in a parlous state owing to the extravagance of his father in building the castle and employing Nash to do it. This was John Trevanion Purnell Bettesworth, born at Caerhays in 1780, who took back the Trevanion name by royal licence in 1801. He was the heir to Sophia's older sister. It is provoking to think that if Sophia had been the elder, Byron would have been the heir to the Cornish estates. As it was, he was quite close to the home of his ancestors when he spent the last week of June 1809 waiting for the Lisbon packet to sail; but though he crossed the harbour to St Mawes, he went no farther up the coast; he found other, more exciting entertainments in the seaport.

The senior branch at Caerhays was staggering dizzily to something like ruin. The Cornish tradition is that Nash tried the experiment of *papiermâché* for roofing, so that the rain poured in; an expensive wall to hold up the hillside garden collapsed and had to be rebuilt.

I happen to possess the auction-catalogue of the Trevanion estates when they were put up for sale. One of the manors was up in the moorland behind St Austell; in time it turned out to be solid china clay – they would have made a million out of it! John Bettesworth Trevanion left the home of his ancestors and died – in some shame, I hope – in Brussels in 1840. Out of the proceeds the family managed to continue, but dispersed. His eldest son married a Trelawny Brereton; *his* son married Lady Frances Bowes-Lyon, daughter of Lord Glamis – Queen Victoria raised her to the rank of an earl's daughter. The family continued, but the lands had gone for ever.

Some driblets of money came through from Augusta to Medora, but not enough for her and Henry to live abroad in any comfort or security. Medora thought of giving herself up to religion and renouncing the flesh; she entered a convent near Carhaix in the hope that 'I might in some way be able to conceal the delicate state of my health, which forbade the hope that the child would live.' When the abbess found out Medora's condition she had to find other accommodation outside. On 19 May 1834 a daughter was born and registered as Marie Violette Trevanion. This child lived to witness her mother's odd fate and, after her death, retreated to a convent at St Germain where she had been educated.

Meanwhile Henry's parent was on the warpath, regarding Medora as responsible for leading him astray. Henry's uncle was dispatched to Carhaix, only to find that the birds had flown. They had found refuge in an old tumbledown *château* called Penhoet, near Morlaix. Medora wrote blissfully, 'we continued to live in a secret and unfrequented spot. Henry at this time gave himself up wholly to religion and shooting; I to my child'.

At home all this led to mutual recriminations between Augusta and the Trevanions. Henry's father could allow him only £450 a year, while Augusta was left to support Georgey and her three little girls as best she could. None of them seemed to have any money-sense – unlike Byron and Annabella. The strain of it all made Medora seriously ill, in addition to which she was denying Henry her bed after her conventual experience. This was more than the Trevanion temperament could stand: he took to a mistress, while Medora took her case to a local doctor. To the local people there was a mystery about the couple, with their aristocratic looks and manners in such squalid circumstances. Medora told her story to the sympathetic doctor who got in touch with her grand relations. This made Henry mad – and jealous too: he suspected the doctor's intentions, both sexual and financial – so like Henry, himself neurotic and over-sensitive. There was a breach; Medora was virtually destitute. After a decade of mingled passion and misery the affair was at an end. What was Medora to do?

At this juncture Lady Byron came forward as a *dea ex machina*. She was now forty-eight – Ada, her daughter by Byron, happily married; Annabella had time and money on her hands, had never ceased to love Byron, lived in the shadow of his memory, with a kind of love-hate fascination for the Byronic. Moreover, she longed for love; she proposed that Medora should live with her.

Unfortunately no one could love Annabella. The experiment was a failure. The only good thing that resulted from it was Medora's friendship with Ada, who treated her as a sister. In spite of all the comforts and security of life with Lady Byron, Medora wanted only to fly out of the gilded cage. She insisted on going back to France; Lady Byron insisted on putting her in charge of a couple of servants: she obviously had no confidence in Medora's being able to manage for herself.

The odd end of her story is not my subject. She ultimately took the bit between her teeth, married a French soldier who fell in love with her, lived the life of a peasant with him, produced a son and died a couple of years after, in 1849, still only thirty-five.

And what of the Trevanions?

It is difficult to trace their story – I should like to know so much more. At some point after the sale of Caerhays Henry was enabled to buy a property in Brittany, at Botives. After the death of her second daughter Georgey decided to try life once more with him, now leading a lonely existence. Henry could get on with neither his wife nor his daughters, who came back to England. Never very strong, evidently as neurotic as Medora, he died alone on Christmas day 1854 in Brittany; he was fifty. Georgey now inherited his share of the Trevanion estate and was at last independent. In 1858 the eldest daughter died at thirty-two.

Everything – except marriage – came to the youngest daughter Ada, called after her cousin, Byron's legitimate daughter. By Byron's will she came into the reversion of his estate to Augusta – a substantial fortune of £28,000 in those days. Half of her total fortune she left to one of her Trevanion cousins when she died in 1882, the rest to Augusta's youngest son.

She, too, like her father was something of a poet – I think a better one. In 1858 *Poems by Ada Trevanion* appeared, undeservedly without notice. The leaves of the Bodleian copy were uncut, I found: no one had read the book. The verses were not to be disconsidered; they have a melancholy charm, more influenced by Tennyson than by her Byron. 'The Old Farmhouse' has the Mariana theme of a girl deserted by her lover, and even the echo –

'The ripe fruit dropped from the garden wall'.

Another echoes Tennyson's May Queen. A lesser Christian Rossetti, she seems to have had an unfulfilled life, having given her love to a young man —

> one among the many brave
> Slain for their country's fame.

Perhaps he was killed in the Crimean War? — how much one would like to know.

But in all the charming book — a more substantial affair than her father's — there is no citation, as in his, of the overwhelming name in the family story; no murmur of all those hectic memories; no references to the familiar places. For, with her generation, the Trevanions were totally uprooted from Caerhays and Cornwall, where they had figured for so long.

2 BYRON'S PROSE*

John D. Jump

Biographers of Byron have drawn freely on his letters and journals. They have used them to give substance to their narratives and to support particular interpretations of his career. While doing so, they have occasionally praised them for their extraordinary vigour and liveliness. Attracted by what they say and what they quote, many readers have turned to the letters and journals for entertainment and illumination.

Yet very few writers have tried to define the nature of their appeal. Professor G. Wilson Knight published a lecture on Byron's prose many years ago, and more recently I have myself devoted a chapter to the subject in my *Byron* (1972). But most of those who are interested in Byron seem still to regard his letters and journals as a mass of autobiographical documents which happen to make entertaining reading rather than as a body of writings with some claim to the kind of attention we normally reserve for more deliberate literary works.

There is little that is deliberate about these writings, which form almost the whole of Byron's extant prose. His friend Thomas Moore, the Irish lyrist, gives us a glimpse of his practice as a correspondent. Punctilious about acknowledging letters, he made a

---

* The standard collections of Byron's prose were for a long time R. E. Prothero's six-volume edition of *Letters and Journals* (London, 1898–1901) and J. Murray's two-volume edition of *Lord Byron's Correspondence* (London, 1922). These are now being superseded by L. A. Marchand's edition of *Byron's Letters and Journals* (London, 1973–   ). Since Marchand prints the letters without cuts, I have used his text as far as it was available at the time of writing and have taken a proportionately large number of my quotations from letters written early enough for him already to have included them. My essay contains a few passages taken from a review contributed to the *Times Literary Supplement*. I am grateful to the Editor for permission to use these.

habit of answering them as soon as he received them. Moore rightly observes that this gave his correspondence 'all the aptitude and freshness of replies in conversation' (*Prose and Verse* (London [1878]) p. 421).

Surviving manuscripts suggest that he wrote rapidly, even impetuously, though perhaps not always as fast as on 4 January 1821. A diary entry of that date records: 'Wrote five letters in about half an hour, short and savage, to all my rascally correspondents.' Irritation and impatience with the dilatoriness of others cannot have improved a handwriting that he himself confessed was 'a sad scrawl' (26 September 1811), even a 'detestable scrawl' (12 April 1814).

A man who could scribble five letters, even if only short ones, in about half an hour naturally wrote a vast number during his lifetime. Moreover, Byron spent most of his adult life far away from his closest British friends. For two years, from 1809 to 1811, he was touring the Mediterranean and living in Greece and Turkey; and he spent his last eight years in self-imposed exile, at first in Switzerland, subsequently and for a much longer period in Italy, and finally in Greece. His absences made regular letter-writing essential if he was to keep in touch with his publisher, his solicitor, his relatives, and his friends and acquaintances. His travels also gave him much to report.

A few figures will suggest the bulk of the material that concerns us. R. E. Prothero edited nearly 1200 of Byron's letters in 1898–1901; a roughly similar number have been published in whole or in part in books or periodicals since then; and Professor L. A. Marchand expects that his edition, which began to appear in 1973, will contain about 3000 when completed. Some of these are brief notes on matters which would nowadays be settled by telephone. But most of them are communications of some substance.

Their most conspicuous quality is their spontaneity. Never, we feel, can written utterance have been less premeditated, less rehearsed, less inhibited, less controlled. Even his complaints of boredom and depression become exuberant. When the ship that was bringing him home after his two-year Mediterranean grand tour was becalmed off Cape St Vincent, he described himself in words taken from Oliver Goldsmith's *The Good-natur'd Man* as 'dull as the last new Comedy'. Admittedly, the ship's captain was a gentlemanly and pleasant man and a courageous officer, 'but as I have got all the particulars of his late action out of him, I don't know what to ask *him* next any more than *you*.' He pauses wearily, then directs against an egotistical fellow-passenger the irritation that has accumulated during the long, tedious days:

> we are infested in the Cabin by another passenger, a teller of tough [that is, tall] stories, all about himself, I could laugh at him were there any body to laugh with, as it is, I yawn and swear to myself, & take refuge in the quarter Gallery [a kind of balcony with windows projecting from the ship's quarter], thank God he is now asleep, or I should be worried with impertinence.

Byron was writing to his old friend and travelling companion John Cam Hobhouse, and it was natural to suppose that by now Hobhouse was asking who this fellow-passenger was and how he came to be on board:

> His name is Thomas and he is Staff or *Stuff* [that is, quack-medicine] Apothecary to Genl. Oakes [commanding the troops at Malta], who has rammed him down our throats for the voyage, and a bitter Bolus [that is, great pill] he is, that's the truth on't.

The pun on 'Staff', the metaphor of ramming down a great pill, and the concluding asseveration show Byron giving a humorous twist to his resentment. He cannot keep it up, however:

> But I long for land, and then for a post-chaise, and I believe my enjoyments will end there, for I have no other pleasure to expect, that I know of.

No doubt Hobhouse was asking whether the whole voyage had been as bad as this. 'We have had a tedious passage,' Byron assures him and then employs a ludicrous analogy to characterise the single livelier spell:

> ... a tedious passage, all except the Straits [of Gibraltar] where we had an Easterly Gale, and glided through the Gut like an oil Glyster.

A gut is a narrow passage of water, such as the Straits; but it is also the bowels, which can easily admit an oil glyster or enema. Having allowed himself this grotesque jest, Byron fears that it may have disconcerted the level-headed and conventional friend of whom he was so fond:

> Dear Hobby, you must excuse all this facetiousness which I should not have let loose, if I knew what the Devil to do, but I am so out of Spirits, & hopes, & humour, & pocket, & health, that you must bear with my merriment, my only resource against a Calenture [that is, a seaman's fever and delirium].

Even here, the catalogue, 'out of Spirits, & hopes, & humour, & pocket, & health', remains humorous; and the exasperated colloquialism, 'if I knew what the Devil to do', like the earlier, 'that's the truth on't', discourages too solemn a view of the depression which again prevails as he ends the letter:

> Write to me, I am now going to patrole the melancholy deck, God be w'ye! yrs. alway, B.—

In this letter, humour and dejection, cordiality and irritation, exasperation and boredom, all achieve utterance in easy and rapid succession one to another. Byron writes as if he were actually engaged in frank and spontaneous talk with his friend, even to the extent of anticipating the questions Hobhouse would naturally ask and answering them at once.

He dated this letter 19 June 1811. Five months later, on 16 November, he had a more eventful matter to report to Hobhouse. His friend the Rev. Robert Bland had asked him to carry a challenge to an officer of Dragoons who was the clergyman's rival for the affections of the promiscuous Susan C. Byron managed to adjust things peaceably. Ten years later he was to recall how difficult this had been, mainly owing to the unhelpful obstinacy of Susan C., 'the d——st b——h that I ever saw, and I have seen a great many' ('Detached Thoughts', 36). Another friend, the 'Sentimental & Sensibilitous' Francis Hodgson (29 June 1811), not yet a clergyman but due to be ordained shortly, had also patronised Susan C. for a while. In his report to Hobhouse, Byron is hardheaded, positive, pugnacious, exuberant, and scornful. Though his mood does not fluctuate as in the letter from on board ship, there can be no doubting the spontaneity of the crescendo of indignant mirth which shapes his account. Having introduced his dramatis personae, he plays briskly on 'life' and 'living' and proceeds to suggest Bland's lunacy by a series of extravagant comparisons:

> Bland (the *Revd*) has been *challenging* an officer of Dragoons, about a *whore*, & my assistance being required, I interfered in time to prevent him from losing his *life* or his *Living*. —The man is mad, Sir, mad, frightful as a Mandrake [a plant with a forked root resembling the human form; it was said to shriek when plucked up], & lean as a rutting Stag [that is, a stag during the mating season], & all about a bitch not worth a Bank token.

This glance at a recent monetary innovation precedes an equally topical reference to a spectacular comet visible in 1811. The malign influence of this comet, and nothing else, can explain the madness of the men involved with Susan C.:

> She is a common Strumpet as his Antagonist assured me, yet he means to marry her, Hodgson meant to marry her, the officer meant to marry her, her first Seducer (seventeen years ago) meant to marry her, and all this is owing to the *Comet*!

Perhaps Hobhouse was wondering how Hodgson came to be one of her suitors. Byron tells him:

> During Bland's absence, H[odgso]n was her Dragon, & left his

own Oyster wench to offer her his hand, which she *refused*.

Catastrophe has ensued. Bland and Hodgson have lapsed from mutual admiration into open enmity:

> Bland comes home in Hysterics, finds her in keeping [that is, living as a kept woman] (not by H[odgso]n however) & loses his wits.—Hodgson gets drunk & cries, & he & Bland (who have been berhyming each other as you know these six past Olympiads) are now the Antipodes of each other.

What kind of woman can she have been who inspired these passions? A ruthless, curt evaluation concludes Byron's report:

> I saw this *wonder*, & set her down at seven shilling's worth.

Rough, candid, steady affection linked Byron and Hobhouse. In the context of their friendship, the spectacle of sentimentalism and folly supplied by Bland and Hodgson naturally provoked impetuous plain speech. But Byron's speech becomes even plainer and more forthright when he continues the story in a letter dated 15 December 1811 to William Harness, a younger man whose protector he had been at Harrow; and he now allows a clearer note of moral disapproval to accompany his ridicule. Bland's conduct is reprehensible in a clergyman and absurd in a man who gives himself the airs of a romantic, pastoral lover:

> Bland is ill of a Gonorrhea, a clerical & creditable distemper, particularly to a despairing Corydon. —Hodgson I should conjecture to have a Syphilis at least, if I may judge by his querulous letter. —So much for these Sentimentalites who console themselves in the stews [that is, the brothel] for the loss, the never to be recovered loss, the despair, of the refined attachment of a brace of Drabs [that is, whores]!

Such an outburst from a man of far from immaculate reputation would no doubt surprise the twenty-one-year-old student he was addressing. So Byron tries to justify it by reminding Harness that he speaks of men who are his elders and whose vocation entitles him to hope that they will prove his betters:

> When I compare myself with these men my Elders & my Betters, I really begin to conceive myself a monument of prudence, a walking statue without feeling or failing. – And yet the World in general hath given me a proud preeminence over them in profligacy.

At the same time, Bland and Hodgson are Byron's friends, and he is not going to deny his regard for them; moreover, there is no concealing his own sexual irregularities:

> Yet I like the men, & God knows, ought not to condemn their aberrations, but I own I feel provoked when they dignify all this with ye. name of love, & deify their common Strumpets.

Friendship does not suffice, however, to silence his condemnation, and a further outburst of indignant ridicule terminates the account:

> Romantic attachments for things marketable at a dollar! – Their Ladies may be averaged at a token each, I believe they have been bought cheaper.

Just as the letter from on board ship swung between depression and facetiousness, so this letter swings between derisive condemnation of Bland and Hodgson and easy-going reluctance to judge them. Thanks to Byron's freedom from inhibition, contradictory moods and attitudes find expression throughout his prose, and his relative indifference to consistency permits him to leave them in open conflict. Byron was not one of those who assume that a truthful statement is one that coheres with other truthful statements. He believed that a truthful statement is one that corresponds with observable facts. But the facts themselves contradict one another. So who can rightly blame him if his statements contradict one another, too? Even in his poetic masterpiece, *Don Juan*, he leaves us wondering whether nature is beneficent or remorseless, whether men are mere beasts or potentially something closer to the angels, and whether there can be a genuine love that is not a guilty love. Observable facts support contradictory answers to all of these questions. So Byron adopts each answer in turn as its truth comes home to him. In xv. lxxxvii, he asks outright:

> . . . if a writer should be quite consistent,
> How could he possibly show things existent?

Naturally, he is more relaxed in his correspondence than in his poetry. Writing with the utmost fidelity to the mood and to the thought of each passing moment, he there reveals himself with little or no reserve. That tedious sea voyage of 1811 plunged him into depression, and he described himself as 'in bitter bad spirits, skies foggy, head muzzy, Capt. sulky, ship lazy' (2 July 1811). The neatness and compactness of the eight words in which he accounts for his condition invite us to smile at it. Yet his gloom is genuine and of a kind that could lead in him to a craving for sensation. He voices this craving again and again. Commenting to Moore upon the unadventurous and provincial lives of 'these Scotch and Lake troubadours', he exclaims:

> Lord, Lord, if these home-keeping minstrels had crossed your Atlantic or my Mediterranean, and tasted a little open boating in a white squall – or a gale in 'the Gut' – or the 'Bay of Biscay,' with no gale at all – how it would enliven and introduce them to a few of the sensations! – to say nothing of an illicit amour or two upon shore, in the way of essay upon the Passions, beginning with simple adultery, and compounding it as they went along.
>
> (3 August 1814)

This is not the only place where an impatient protest issues in humour. Talk with his father-in-law prompts a complaint of 'that damned monologue, which elderly gentlemen call conversation' (8 March 1815); and a less specific irritation leads him to declare,

'All men are intrinsical rascals, and I am only sorry that, not being a dog, I can't bite them' (20 October 1821). Nor is he slow to direct his mockery against himself: 'my mind's made up, positively fixed, determined, and therefore I will listen to reason, because now it can do no harm' (20 September 1814). The decision in question related to his disastrous marriage.

He writes soberly and earnestly, however, when he addresses Lord Holland, the leader of the moderate Whigs in the House of Lords, about the Nottinghamshire weavers whose desperate recourse to Luddite violence the Tory government planned to check by making frame-breaking a capital offence. 'I have seen the state of these miserable men,' he declares, '& it is a disgrace to a civilized country. – Their excesses may be condemned, but cannot be subject of wonder. – The effect of ye. present bill would be to drive them into actual rebellion' (25 February 1812). This was to be the theme of his maiden speech in the House of Lords two days later. Byron is equally serious in his commitment to the cause of a free Italy. Living in an area dominated by the Austrians, he snatches at an opportunity of cocking a snook at the imperial censorship:

> I could have sent you a good deal of Gossip and some *real* information, were it not that all letters pass through the Barbarians' inspection, and I have no wish to inform *them* of any thing but my utter abhorrence of them and theirs. They have only conquered by treachery, however.
>
> (19 May 1821)

An earlier act of impudence shows him in a much more cheerful and high-spirited vein. Writing from the Dardanelles, he devotes three sentences to comparing the Turks and the English. The first minimises the differences. The second contrasts the fashionable vices in the two nations, alliteration emphasising that particular Turkish taste which the English find most outrageous. The third sentence, briefly applauding the Turks, comes impudently close to applauding that most outrageous vice:

I see not much difference between ourselves & the Turks, save that we have foreskins and they none, that they have long dresses and we short, and that we talk much and they little. – In England the vices in fashion are whoring & drinking, in Turkey, Sodomy & smoking, we prefer a girl and a bottle, they a pipe and pathic. – They are sensible people.

(3 May 1810)

With a similar cheerful impudence, he mocks his own susceptibility to the attentions of Marianna Segati: 'her great merit is finding out mine – there is nothing so amiable as discernment' (25 November 1816).

Byron's letters are remarkable for their freshness, their unhesitating, uncensored response to the immediate situation. Many of them are gay, mocking, irreverent. Even when his recurrent melancholy weighs heavily upon him, he remains capable of asserting himself humorously against it. Sometimes he writes earnestly and purposefully. On such occasions, his humour may manifest itself as grim or savage satire. Whatever his mood, his correspondence exhibits an unfailing exuberance and vigour. Inconsistencies among his attitudes and opinions do not trouble him. If each of two incompatible positions seems to him to be tenable, he occupies both and cheerfully laughs off the contradiction.

He seems always to write with his correspondent vividly in mind. To Hobhouse his manner is frank, hearty, forthright, and trenchant. While he never quite forgets that he is an aristocrat and John Murray a tradesman, he soon comes to address his publisher as a respected friend. His warm fondness for Moore finds frequent and very cordial expression. A slightly patronising playfulness enlivens his affectionate letters to his half-sister, Augusta. A similar tone makes itself felt in his early letters to young Harness; for example, he parodies the kind of advice that most men think age authorises them to dispense to their juniors:

Now, Child, what art thou doing? *reading I trust*. I want to see you take a degree, remember this is the most important period of your life, & don't disappoint your Papa & your Aunts & all your kin, besides myself, don't you know that all male children were begotten for the express purpose of being Graduates?

(8 December 1811)

Contrasting in some respects with these are the urbane, witty, and sharply observant letters he wrote to Lady Melbourne, an older woman who was his honorary 'aunt' during his years of fame in England. His reports to her on his involvement with the Wedderburn Websters during 1812–13 shape themselves into a sparkling little comedy of manners.

Every characteristic letter of Byron's is accurately adapted for its particular recipient. Equally, it springs directly from the unique situation in which he wrote it. A good example from the later part of his life is the letter he wrote to Moore on 8 March 1822. At the end of the previous year he had published *Cain*, a dramatic poem in which the hero's romantic rebellion culminates in open blasphemy. Byron insisted that the blasphemy was Cain's and Lucifer's, not his own. But many readers were understandably offended; the work seemed to them to be objectionable both theologically and politically.

Meanwhile, Byron was growing impatient with John Murray. The publisher's fear of Tory reviewers and Tory customers was making him dilatory in issuing the more recent cantos of *Don Juan*, and Byron was thinking of severing their business connection. Moore evidently warned him against acting precipitately and then grew afraid that this advice had given offence. Byron opens his letter by allaying his friend's anxiety. With a touch of self-mockery he declares that he has already 'pacified' himself and 'subsided back to Albemarle Street', where Murray's premises stood. He explains that 'vacillation, occasional neglect, and troublesome sincerity [that is, frank but unacceptable criticism]', such as he has suffered from Murray, are quite enough 'to put your truly great author and man into a passion'. But, having reflected, he has regained his composure. Abruptly dropping his comic manner, he pays an earnest tribute to his friend:

I really feel ashamed of having bored you so frequently and fully of late. But what could I do? You are a friend – an absent one, alas! – and as I trust no one more, I trouble you in proportion.

He then turns to *Cain* and the consequent outcry from the devout. The convent education provided for his illegitimate daughter, Allegra, proves him 'a great admirer of tangible religion'. Praise of the Roman Catholic faith follows. But his appreciation of it is merely aesthetic; and he lets slip that there is a pagan religion which he finds even more elegant. Such praise will gratify no Christian.

This war of 'Church and State' has astonished me more than it disturbs; for I really thought *Cain* a speculative and hardy, but still a harmless, production. As I said before, I am really a great admirer of tangible religion; and am breeding one of my daughters a Catholic, that she may have her hands full. It is by far the most elegant worship, hardly excepting the Greek mythology. What with incense, pictures, statues, altars, shrines, relics, and the real presence, confession, absolution,—there is something sensible to grasp at. Besides, it leaves no possibility of doubt; for those who swallow their Deity, really and truly, in transubstantiation, can hardly find any thing else otherwise than easy of digestion.

He must have wondered whether he had gone too far in the reckless jest with which he ends this paragraph. After all, Moore had been brought up as a Catholic. So Byron concludes his letter on a note of reassurance and at the same time confesses to his ungovernable impulse to take even the most serious matters 'in the absurd point of view':

I am afraid that this sounds flippant, but I don't mean it to be so; only my turn of mind is so given to taking things in the absurd point of view, that it breaks out in spite of me every now and then. Still, I do assure you that I am a very good Christian. Whether you will believe me in this, I do not know; but I trust you will take my word for being

'Very truly and affectionately' yours, etc.

His claim to be 'a very good Christian' presumably means no more than that he is a person of charitable disposition. He intends the claim to balance his ironically equivocal praise of religion and his jocular and blasphemous suggestion that if Roman Catholics can swallow their God they can swallow anything. Above all, he wishes his letter to communicate to Moore his heartfelt regard for a friend whom he sorely misses in his Italian exile. As in his earlier letters, he is giving immediate and spontaneous utterance to the feelings inspired by his correspondent and by the situation in which he finds himself. Thomas Moore, the outcry against *Cain*, and his business connection with John Murray can inspire irreconcilable feelings. He voices all of them, irreconcilable or not.

What prevents such letters from lapsing into incoherence? Part of the answer is implicit in what I have already said. Byron writes with the distinctive individuality of each correspondent so vividly in mind, and his letters spring with such directness from his actual situation, that they automatically take the shape determined by that situation and by his relationship with the person addressed. But even more important in giving his letters coherence and form is the personality of the man himself. From his letters and journals generally, he emerges – if I may quote what I have myself written elsewhere – as 'impulsive and exuberant; humorous and observant; liable to moods of profound dejection from which he seeks relief in violent excitement; enamoured of action; and proud and spirited in his hatred of oppression'. Such a man, speaking to others whom he enables us to imagine, and reacting to situations which he enables us to envisage, gives us letters that approximate again and again to the condition of dramatic monologues.

But what of his journals or diaries? The documents generally classified as such are principally four in number. The first runs from the autumn of 1813 to the spring of 1814, a period when Byron was enjoying great fame in England but was troubled by his involvement in an especially awkward 'scrape'. The second records his experiences and reflections during a tour of the Bernese Alps shortly after the failure of his marriage and the start of his self-inflicted exile; he wrote this for Augusta, and it is best regarded as a letter in many instalments. The third covers the first two months of 1821, when Byron was living in the palazzo of Count Guiccioli, the husband of his mistress Teresa Guiccioli, and awaiting a call to arms with the Italian nationalists. The fourth, begun later in the same year, is not a journal or diary at all but a collection of 'Detached Thoughts', preceded by a few pages of 'My Dictionary'. Two journals that he opened during the Greek adventure which was to cost him his life came to so little that we may ignore them.

In his journals, Byron has naturally no opportunity of exhibiting that astute awareness of each individual correspondent that delights us in the letters. At the same time, he does not seem in his journals to be writing merely for himself. The journal of the tour in the Bernese Alps is a special case, of course, since he compiled it deliberately for Augusta. But even in the journals of 1813–14 and 1821 he appears to have an audience in view. A writer who wished merely to put something on record for his own interest would surely make less use of the oaths and exclamations, repetitions, parentheses, and abrupt halts which have the effect of projecting Byron dramatically upon his readers' imaginations. Since he certainly did not write his journals for immediate publication, any audience that he had in mind must have belonged to posterity. Judging by the tone and feeling of his journals, he must have imagined it as composed preponderantly of men like his friends Hobhouse, Murray, Moore, and Kinnaird.

Each of the two really extensive journals or diaries has a background of political events of lively interest to Byron himself. While he was writing that of 1813–14, Napoleon was going under for the first time. He fought a series of skilful defensive battles, but the Allies forced him back on Paris, and in the spring of 1814 he abdicated. 'What strange tidings', Byron writes several months before the end,

> from that Anakim [that is, giant; Byron having mistaken the Hebrew plural for a singular] of anarchy – Buonaparte! Ever since I defended my bust of him at Harrow against the rascally

time-servers, when the war broke out in 1803, he has been a *Héros de Roman* of mine – on the Continent; I don't want him here. But I don't like those same flights – leaving of armies, etc., etc. I am sure when I fought for his bust at school, I did not think he would run away from himself. But I should not wonder if he banged them yet. To be beat by men would be something; but by three stupid, legitimate-old-dynasty boobies of regular-bred sovereigns [of Russia, Prussia, and Austria] –

(17 November 1813)

and he breaks off into lamentations. Six days later, he feels disappointment that Napoleon, instead of bringing down everything in his fall, is simply being 'pared away to gradual insignificance'. Here we are, he complains, 'retrograding, to the dull, stupid old system, – balance of Europe – poising straws upon kings' noses, instead of wringing them off!' On 18 February 1814, he feels that matters have reached a crisis. 'Napoleon! – this week will decide his fate. All seems against him; but I believe and hope he will win – at least, beat back the invaders.' As if in fulfilment of his hope, the report reaches him before the end of the month that 'Buonaparte is not yet beaten; but has rebutted Blucher, and repiqued Schwartzenburg' (27 February 1814). A week later, he writes defiantly and triumphantly: 'Sent my fine print of Napoleon to be framed. It *is* framed; and the Emperor becomes his robes as if he had been hatched in them' (6 March 1814).

But the battles of Nangis and Montereau did not halt the Allied advance. On 8 April 1814, Byron finds 'my poor little pagod [that is, idol], Napoleon, pushed off his pedestal; – the thieves are in Paris.' Napoleon, however, 'is in their rear – between them and their homes. Query – will they ever reach them?' On the following day, even this faint hope dies. 'Napoleon Buonaparte has abdicated the throne of the world. . . . What! wait till they were in his capital, and then talk of his readiness to give up what is already gone! ! . . . I am utterly bewildered and confounded.' Ten days later, on 19 April 1814, he concludes the journal by recording '"that the Bourbons are restored! ! !" – "Hang up philosophy." To be sure, I have long despised myself and man, but I never spat in the face of my species before – "O fool! I shall go mad."'

For Byron, the political crisis accompanies a personal crisis. During the last months of 1813 and the early part of 1814 his personal relationships were tangled and dangerously irregular. He was unhappy and bored.

The diary of January and February 1821 belongs to a broadly similar phase of lethargy and depression. As in the earlier journal, the stresses of Byron's personal life, and the speculations which these engender, find expression alongside the record of a political crisis. During 1820–1 a wave of revolutionary unrest passed over Europe. In Italy, a movement of national liberation from Austrian imperialism was gathering strength. At the Congress of Troppau (1820) the powers of the reactionary Holy Alliance – Austria, Russia, and Prussia – claimed the right to intervene in the affairs of any country which showed signs of becoming democratic; and on 6 February 1821 an Austrian army crossed the Po and marched south to suppress such a development in Naples. Byron, as one of the Carbonari in Ravenna, hoped that Italian nationalists would take up arms and operate in the invaders' rear. He helped to equip his comrades and was ready to go into action with them. But the Neapolitans collapsed, and the rising which he had expected in his own area did not occur. Like its predecessor of 1813–14, the diary of 1821 ends in political disappointment. At no stage, however, does Byron doubt that the final victory will go to the people. On 13 January 1821 he writes:

> Dined – news come – the *Powers* mean to war with the peoples. The intelligence seems positive – let it be so – they will be beaten in the end. The king-times are fast finishing. There will be blood shed like water, and tears like mist; but the peoples will conquer in the end. I shall not live to see it, but I foresee it.

By dwelling to this extent upon the personal unease and the political disappointment which prevail in both journals, I risk giving a misleading impression of their similarity and of the degree of unity each possesses. Miscellaneity is what we naturally expect in such writings, and it is what Byron gives us. 'This journal is a relief', he writes on 6 December 1813:

> When I am tired – as I generally am – out comes this, and down goes every thing. But I can't read it over; and God knows what contradictions it may contain. If I am sincere with myself (but I fear one lies more to one's self than to any one else), every page should confute, refute, and utterly abjure its predecessor.

Accordingly, he reports current happenings, recalls past events, and reflects upon both; he discusses what he is reading and mentions what he is writing; occasionally, and more especially in the later diary and in 'Detached Thoughts', he ponders psychological and metaphysical questions. He expresses himself as lucidly, as vivaciously, and as racily as in his letters.

On 30 November 1813 he refers to his having dined with Lord Holland two days earlier:

> Why does Lady H. always have that damned screen between the whole room and the fire? I, who bear cold no better than an antelope, and never yet found a sun quite *done* to my taste, was absolutely petrified, and could not even shiver. All the rest, too, looked as if they were just unpacked, like salmon from an icebasket, and set down to table for that day only. When she retired, I watched their looks as I dismissed the screen, and every cheek thawed, and every nose reddened with the anticipated glow.

His delight in the ludicrous can overflow even in the generally sombre journal composed for Augusta in 1816:

> Went to Chillon through Scenery worthy of I know not whom; went over the Castle of Chillon again. On our return met an English party in a carriage; a lady in it fast asleep! – fast asleep in the most anti-narcotic spot in the world – excellent! I remember, at Chamouni, in the very eyes of Mont Blanc, hearing another woman, English also, exclaim to her party 'did you ever see any thing more *rural*?' – as if it was Highgate, or

Hampstead, or Brompton, or Hayes, – '*Rural!*' quotha! Rocks, pines, torrents, Glaciers, Clouds, and Summits of eternal snow far above them – and '*Rural!*' I did not know the thus exclaiming fair one, but she was a very good kind of woman.

(18 September 1816)

In his journals as in his letters, indignation finds expression that is both earnest and comical. While awaiting a call to arms in 1821, he learned that a number of his fellow-Carbonari had gone off on a sporting expedition. A sharp contrast and a ludicrous catalogue convey his scorn:

> The principal persons in the events which may occur in a few days are gone out on a *shooting party*. If it were like a '*highland hunting*', a pretext of the chase for a grand re-union of counsellors and chiefs, it would be all very well. But it is nothing more or less than a real snivelling, popping, small-shot, water-hen waste of powder, ammunition, and shot, for their own special amusement: a rare set of fellows for 'a man to risk his neck with'.

Two days later, on 26 January 1821, he returns to the subject:

> The gentlemen, who make revolutions and are gone on a shooting, are not yet returned. They don't return till Sunday [two days later still] – that is to say, they have been out for five days, buffooning, while the interests of a whole country are at stake, and even they themselves compromised.

The 'Detached Thoughts', compiled later in this same year, are exactly what the title says: thoughts gay and grave, some reminiscent and some speculative, jotted down as they came into his mind. They can be richly absurd, as when he remembers one of the authors who submitted plays with a view to their performance at Drury Lane:

> Mr. O'Higgins, then resident at Richmond, with an Irish tragedy, in which the unities could not fail to be observed, for the

protagonist was chained by the leg to a pillar during the chief part of the performance. He was a wild man, of a salvage appearance; and the difficulty of *not* laughing at him was only to be got over by reflecting upon the probable consequences of such cachinnation.

('Detached Thoughts', 67)

Many of the 'Detached Thoughts' are grave, even gloomy:

If I had to live over again, I do not know what I would change in my life, unless it were *for not to have lived at all*. All history and experience, and the rest, teaches us that the good and evil are pretty equally balanced in this existence, and that what is most to be desired is an easy passage out of it.

('Detached Thoughts', 95)

From here, he moves on to reflections upon immortality, upon the doctrine of eternal punishment, and upon the relationship of body and soul. He considers this last 'a sad jar'.

In journals and letters alike, Byron allows his natural mobility of temperament to reveal itself in rapid and sometimes subversive fluctuations of mood; vigorously and racily, he sets down what he has observed; and he comments wittily, sympathetically, humorously, or mockingly upon whatever has excited his interest. He is one of the most versatile and provocative of our letter-writers and diarists; and more than any other he has left us a collection of writings that constitute a brilliant and incisive self-portrait, above all a dramatic self-portrait, of one whom we can never know too well.

3 THE POET OF *CHILDE HAROLD*

Francis Berry

'*Alles Grosses bildet*', Goethe said of Byron: 'every great *thing* is a portent, an active embodying representation; it is more than a symbol of the moment because it is active, predictive of the future, its immediate agent. Byron was such a thing, an it.' Now that all sounds very one-time German, Goethian and pompous, but not therefore always false. As on many other occasions – this was in December 1816 – Goethe was right.

In 1827, three years after Byron's death, Goethe referred to his *Helena*, that vast Act III of the second part of *Faust*, written in his old age. In that Act, Faust consummates his nuptials with Helen of Greece, and from that union is born Euphorion, whom Goethe acknowledged to be Byron. 'You were right to present him with that immortal monument of love in *The Helena*,' said Eckermann. The younger man was deferential, but he was not a toady. He could have asked: Why, your Excellency, do you attach such importance to the late Lord Byron as to bring him in *Faust*, Part II, as Euphorion? But Goethe explained. For he declared: 'I could not . . . make use of any man as the representative of the modern poetical era except him, who undoubtedly is the greatest genius of our century.' Again Byron is 'neither Antique [classical] nor Romantic but like the present day – itself': to understand, to realise what the moment in 1827 *is*, and what its tomorrow will be, understand and realise what Byron is.

Which is, of this poet if of no other, to realise beyond the poetry and understand the life. Goethe said he had intended a different conclusion to *The Helena*: 'then this conclusion with Lord Byron and Missolonghi was suggested to me by the events of the day

[Byron's death in 1824 in Greece] and I gave up all the rest.' The issue of the marriage between Faust and Helena died in Greece. How luckily for an old and famous author, seeking for a conclusion exactly right for this part of his masterpiece, that this should happen. But it did. And Byron too was lucky that it should happen that he died then and there, perhaps.

A more specifically literary-critical remark by Goethe. Speaking of one of Byron's plays (*The Two Foscari*) he exclaimed: 'Admirable! every word is strong, significant, and subservient to the aim – there are no weak lines in Byron.' No weak lines in 'Byron' – and no waste! But it is possible that he had only this play particularly in mind. In his introduction to *The Two Foscari*, Byron had written: 'The simplicity of plot is intentional and the avoidance of *rant* also, as also the compression of the speeches in the most severe situations.'

Be that as it may, whatever Byron's merits as a poet, as specified by Goethe, they are not surely – except perhaps for 'strong' – the ones recognised in the twentieth century. For T. S. Eliot, until lately our century's representative poet and critic, wrote in 1937:

> Byron would seem the most nearly remote from the sympathies of every living critic . . . The bulk of Byron's verse is distressing in proportion to its quality . . . We have come to expect poetry to be something very concentrated, something distilled; but if Byron had distilled his verse, there would have been nothing whatever left.

Against the 'strong, significant, and subservient to the aim . . . there are no weak lines' (compactness, all meaningful, organic unity, no waste) of Goethe, we have Eliot's: 'Byron has been admired for his most ambitious efforts to be poetic: and these attempts turn out on examination to be fake; nothing but sonorous affirmations of the commonplace.' It can be exactly understood what the Christian critic means: by 1937 the 'sonorous affirmations' had become 'commonplace'. But they had become *déjà vu* to Byron himself when he wrote the stanza which provoked the comment. The affirmations of Gray's *Elegy*, less sonorous, equally publicly addressed, are also commonplace.

The critics between Goethe and Eliot foresaw the weakness, not original but which time has brought; to Matthew Arnold 'Byron was a child as soon as he began to think.' Nevertheless he was the one English poet who realised the essential need for 'action', for 'subject matter', in poetry, and Arnold clearly recognised Byron as in this respect the first poet of – what was still – their shared age. Yes, the Victorians had their reservations, and George Eliot could style Byron 'a vulgar genius'. Of course to her he was vulgar ('a vulgar patrician', T. S. Eliot was to call him), but there was no doubt as to the genius. 'Whereas', as Auden was to remark in his 'Letter to Lord Byron':

> Whereas T. S. Eliot, I am sad to find,
> Damns you with an uninteresting mind.

It is a clash between the poetics and the theologies of two periods. Both twentieth-century poetics and Eliot's theology probably inclined him to admit, even assert, as against the earlier poetry, the merits of *Don Juan*, that great *déjà vu* testament. Here Eliot admits a 'raffish honesty' – Byron could detachedly look at himself – whereas the earlier diabolism and the postures of defiance had been spurious. *Scrutiny* too had exempted (though no theology or merely a very grey one had been involved) *Don Juan* in its dismissal of an *oeuvre*, all largely of a period. We now should recognise *Don Juan* as the one supreme comic poem in English. Even so, of the whole output, early or late, not excluding the comic epic, there is this summarising: 'Of Byron one can say, as of no other English poet of his eminence, that he added nothing to the language, that he discovered nothing in the sound, and develops nothing in the meaning of individual words.' And this verdict: he 'might have been an accomplished foreigner writing in English'. Not much later another critic, an admirable and interesting critic, remote in theology (he had none) and politics, and in poetics, from Eliot, yet near in human sympathies – Herbert Read – was to declare that Byron's verse showed no 'true voice of feeling' unlike Keats's verse, but that Byron's words were poured *ti-tum, ti-tum, ti-tum* into pre-cast frames.

I grew up at a time when Eliot's prestige as a poet approached that of Byron a hundred years earlier, though Eliot's was more hardly won; and when Eliot's criticism (the auxiliary to his poems, and always working towards the making of a 'climate of opinion' favourable to the acceptance of his poems, creating the critical taste necessary for the enjoyment of his own poems) had an extraordinarily persuasive authority, even hold. How could the young man of the early thirties answer such a carefully argued case demonstrating Byron's incapacity for original thought or his insensitivity towards the English language? Or fail to agree with Herbert Read, that Byron's metrics were duly mechanical? There were answers, but what were they? Were there answers without resorting to the Life? Or to the Letters and Journals, so close to the Life but still, then, an under-read and under-appreciated area of the poet's writing?

It can take years before one can outgrow views and opinions conditioned by the views and opinions of the great and respected; to outgrow while still respecting, while gaining an understanding of the reason or reasons for the formation of the views and opinions of the conditioner. In the case of Eliot the views and opinions of the critic were essential – and inevitable – to the growth and maturation of Eliot the poet. To at last understand that; and then to further realise that such views and opinions ought not to govern, either with regard to Byron or to another poet, one's own individual feelings – this is a result of ageing, and a result, too, of noting that the most eminent poet-critics can modify, if not reverse, earlier opinions which their generation and their temperament and their ambitions dictated. This is simply a warning that it is damaging to read, say, an introduction or preface to a collected or a selected edition of a poet unless its writer delights in that poet. Eliot knew this, and his preface to his choice of Kipling serves as an example. Nevertheless, in the *Selected Essays* he drew the young reader towards the Jacobean dramatists; he repelled him from the Romantics. This was perhaps right and necessary at the time – though time is a 'whirligig' – except in so far as it ministered to the pride of belief that it was unnecessary to read

Byron before accepting a judgement on him.

Anyway, it is now 1974, and times have changed for Byron, and Eliot, and for the readers of both. The positive homage of Goethe, the negating strictures of Eliot, respectively, provoke endorsement and expansion or resistance at the present.

In the interim, during the thirties, in a series of letters in the delightfully entertaining *Letters from Iceland* by W. H. Auden and Louis MacNeice, the former, with wit and high-spirited brilliance, saluted, in verses derived from *ottava rima*, the 'inventor' of a style; Byron was 'the master of the airy manner'. And in a volume originally entitled *The Burning Oracle*, but now republished as *Poets of Action*, G. Wilson Knight stood firm as the champion not only of the *Beppo–Don Juan* group but of the whole vast and magnificent Byronic achievement, an achievement that included, but was not confined to, the creation of a poetry which galvanised the poets of several languages of Europe.

To declare my position: I have come, and not a moment too soon, to accept Byron's poetry with enormous pleasure and admiration, and to receive, when I read him, an intense kind of driving excitement, vigour and assurance not found elsewhere in nineteenth-century English poetry. And with what consequence? With this: he alone would seem to combine a propulsive revolutionary blaze, an expanding of sympathies, with an equally strong blaze – or passion – for metrical and stanzaic, and a larger constructional, order. In the present age of fervour but near anarchy in life and in letters, Byron is the wholesome model for poets writing today, and tomorrow. He admired Dryden; he admired Pope. Yet he was liberal; more than that, a liberator; and he understood himself. He can help tomorrow's lives as well as tomorrow's poets.

Byron's drive, vigour, assurance! But 'We have come to expect poetry to be very concentrated, something distilled . . .' And not only concentrated, but diffident – as diffident as Mr Prufrock is diffident. This was generally true of expectations in the 1920s and the 1930s and the 1940s. It would have been agreed that a mind, and its moods, are nearly infinitely subtle, that the language was tired, and that the grand gestures of rhetoric were outdated because they were expressive of certainties, and the educated man, the civilised man (the descendant of Henry James's people), the sensitive man, was incapable of the callow, or shallow; of the untested assumption; of all those forms of rhetoric which could only be the utterance of a crude insensibility – which insensibility was expressive of little except a lack of awareness of the complexities of modern life. Certainties! look for them to Mussolini, for 'The best lack all conviction . . .' while it is 'the worst' who are full 'of passionate intensity'. The poet's job was to be aware of these complexities, of the proper diffidences that attended such awareness, and to render them. That citation from F. H. Bradley, in the Notes to *The Waste Land*, is a sufficient indication that not only the transmutation of an experience but the experience itself, any experience, must be peculiar to the individual. That tree, that bus, is *there*, but to no two among all the millions is it the same tree, the same bus. Or are tree and bus really not there? Realise, then, what a task, a tricky one, it is to write a poem – a genuine one. Or to address others in a common understanding in any mode or mood. 'I gotta use words when I talk to you,' declared the hero, Sweeney. Whether he communicated or not meant 'nothing'.

Hence the *symboliste*, and later the Eliotic, and all the sub- or post-Eliotic postulates, or lack of them, and they companion, or presuppose, most assuredly a profound – a so profound as to be fundamental – scepticism of the worth of heroic action, of 'heroes' and of 'action', of rhetoric or thumping discourse.

Now what are the striking qualities of Byron's verse? So striking, as they were, that they shook London and agitated Europe?

Besides being politically revolutionary with a passion for rigorously stable artistic form and forms, he was, of all poets, 'a man speaking to men'. This was Wordsworth's definition of the poet in the exercise of his office. But with Wordsworth it was a *desideratum*; Byron spoke clearly and boldly not *for* peasants – but *to* all men (and women) with an interest in public affairs, in human behaviour, and with a real or affected interest in what used to be called the passions. Historic events are not superseded by those occurring later. Unashamedly, I quote lines in evidence of this, because they are so well known:

> There was a sound of revelry by night,
> And Belgium's Capital had gathered then
> Her Beauty and her Chivalry – and bright
> The lamps shone o'er fair women and brave men;
> A thousand hearts beat happily; and when
> Music arose with its voluptuous swell,
> Soft eyes looked love to eyes which spake again,
> And all went merry as a marriage-bell;
> But hush! hark! a deep sound strikes like a rising knell!
> *(Childe Harold's Pilgrimage*, III.xxi)

Of course this is rhetoric, or public address; certainly the poet could count on that audience being interested in the Battle of Waterloo, and the hours before that battle. He could take it for granted that the audience were as wholly with him here, as he could take it for granted that there was some opposition when he had used prose oratory in the House of Lords on behalf of the Nottinghamshire stocking-frame breakers. This consciousness and confidence of an audience – in the tradition of Dryden and Pope – sets Byron apart 'from all the Lakers in and out of season' and from Keats. Wordsworth, the recluse, would murmur to himself, 'I wandered lonely as a cloud' (albeit he was with his sister); Keats, in solitariness, assumed a sympathetic overhearer, when *he* murmured about the condition of his heart and his sense:

> My heart aches, and a drowsy numbness pains
> My sense as though of hemlock I had drunk –

but Byron is addressing an assured audience about an event of public importance to the British then and to our partners in the Common Market now. This is not to suggest that Wordsworth or Keats are to be despised (nor indeed that they are either inferior or superior), but it is to point to the strong difference in kind between

Byron and them, and to suggest why Byron did, to some degree, genuinely look down on them. He, like Keats, to be sure complained about his heart, indeed paraded 'the pageant of his bleeding heart' across Europe, but he related those pangs to the settings of historical events that fairly claimed the interest of his assured audience in London and in the countries of Europe. He made the landscapes of Europe vivid and vibrative with memories for the Europeans. He became, and still is, the Common Market poet. He displayed an interest in Europe, and Europe has repaid the compliment, as Wilson Knight pointed out: but since 'Common' has its demeaning significance ('a common lodging house'), let us say he is the poet of Our Shared Europe. Along with insurance, freight charges and capital investments, Byron ranks high among our 'invisible exports', however deplorable the figures of our balance of trade. But, of course, he shared himself particularly with Italy and with Greece.

We can notice, in that 'eve before the Battle of Waterloo' stanza, its lucidity combined with, or in despite of, its packing of detail – detail observed, detail heard. It has the Byronic charge, the drive of confidence. He composed hurriedly, chancing the luck of his enormous talent. Well, he had luck, and could justify his aristocratic contempt for those who toiled, strained and revised in composition. He possessed the Renaissance *sprezzatura*. And he could manage the swell – and the check. And he had a virtuosity in the management of stops. The whole rising surge of social grand ballroom gaiety is checked by that last line which is, appropriately, an alexandrine 'dragging its slow length along'. The stanza is a prescription for a score of historical painters submitting their pictures of 'the night before Waterloo.'

In the happy violence of such verse, Byron has re-tuned the Spenserian stanza to suit his own nature. The stanza in *The Faerie Queene*, for all its grace, was disposed to languor, moving, as Coleridge expressed it, 'with the moon's soft pace', a stanza with a pulse beat agreeable to Thomson's celebration of lassitude in *The Castle of Indolence* but remote from the strength and pace of the Byronic pulse. Traces of this inherited languor and distancing are discernible in the early stanzas of *Childe Harold*, with their slowing and softening 'sooths to say', their 'wights', 'hights' and 'swains', and the stanza, on account of its name (what other stanza is named after its founder?), and its original purpose – pilgrimages, questing knights or apprentice knights – provided Byron with the bold 'plan'. And as he acquired the knack (as later he was to acquire the knack of the *ottava rima* and then transform that) he came to subdue it to his own masterful temperament, to direct it. Still a connection between the two poets remains because of that stanza. Following *Childe Harold*, Shelley and Keats wrote poems in the Spenserian stanza. They are derivatives of *Childe Harold*'s fame more than Spenser's. *The Faerie Queene* and Byron's poem are connected but contrasted: each expresses its age. In this way they were both originals and epoch-making.

In *The Faerie Queene* it is the spiritual contests and the interior landscapes that primarily signify, but in *Childe Harold* it is the outward, veritable, evidential fact that is registered – the fact in the past, the fact in the now – and signifies. And let the observer, the knower, digest it as he can, adjusting his sensibility's capacity to absorb the shock. Hence no apology again for invoking the bullfight which fascinates the British tourists today in their thousands, even as they condemn it, as it did the few travellers who watched it in 1809. The poet, early tourist (and it is here, I suspect, that the poet first positively breaks with the 'slow pace' of Spenser, whose jousting knights are seen in slow motion through shimmering gauze), hears:

> Hushed is the din of tongues . . .

and sees:

> on gallant steeds . . .
> Four cavaliers prepare . . .

The picadors' lances are to break the muscles of the neck so that the matador may finally confront the exhausted animal with its head lowered sufficiently for him to poise and bring his blade down vertically to the heart. Next Byron observes that the peons with their athletic nimbleness have planted their 'clinging' darts with ribbons or streamers attached to weaken and enrage; have skipped out of the way just in time.

> On foams the Bull, but not unscathed he goes;
> Streams from his flank the crimson torrent clear;
> He flies, he wheels, distracted with his throes;
> Dart follows dart; . . .

A horse, carrying a lancer, is gored and 'unseamed appears':

> His gory chest unveils life's panting source . . .

The horse is down on its haunches, but it gets up:

> Though death-struck, still his feeble frame he rears:
> Staggering, but stemming all, his Lord [his rider]
> unharmed he bears.

The matador makes his kill:

> Where his vast neck just mingles with the spine,
> Sheathed in his form the deadly weapon lies.
> He [the bull] stops – he starts – disdaining to decline:
> Slowly he falls, amidst triumphant cries . . .

The carcass needs to be cleared from the ring before the next fight, the sand must be spread over the blood, so

> The decorated car appears – on high
> The corse is piled – sweet sight for vulgar eyes –
> Four steeds that spurn the rein, as swift as shy,
> Hurl the dark bulk along, scarce seen in dashing by.

The poet, and he is a young poet, has made vividly real in words the drama (but is that the word since a drama runs to a preordained text?), or sport, or high ceremony, of the bullfight. And since he was in Spain he could scarcely have done otherwise than poetically realise – act by act, or round by round – a ceremony which, in its blood-spill, passion, excitement and skill, is so poignantly eloquent of the country. And rereading the stanzas (*Childe Harold's Pilgrimage*, I. lxxii–lxxx), I find it evident how open Byron was, and how he shared, like a good poet, the experience: the excitement, the passion, the blood, the death – consequences of daring skill. Yet, also like a good poet, because he is of inclusive sympathies, after giving himself to the experience, vivid and gleaming with violence, he could, absorbing it, judge that the 'sport' was 'ungentle':

> Such the ungentle sport that oft invites
> The Spanish maid, and cheers the Spanish swain . . .

But 'ungentle' the grandees and dames? The *thing*, the event or ceremony, requires an explanation, and this is to be had by recourse to the Spaniard's history; his genius (if so it can be called) for 'pain' must be referred to the *vendetta*:

> Nurtured in blood betimes, his heart delights
> In vengeance, gloating on another's pain . . .

No excuse, we say, to be case-hardened to cruelty. No excuse, but an attempt at an understanding. Where else, but by an investigation of the past, of history, can we obtain an understanding which is sympathetic, not indictory?

Here it is opportune to remark on Byron's use of words. Eliot, we recall, charged Byron with 'an imperceptiveness to the English word', and Auden referred to 'his lack of reverence for words'; and Byron's wife (none other, as Auden notes) declared that her husband used words 'as Bonaparte did lives, for conquest without regard to their value'.

All poets 'use words' – in different ways. If Byron used words to sway the large and important audience he commanded, and which he succeeded in swaying, then he was honourably exercising poetic rhetoric as have other great poets of the past. In the following lines,

> Four steeds that spurn the rein, as swift as shy,
> Hurl the dark bulk along, scarce seen in dashing by,

there are four syntactic units, 'Four . . . rein', 'as . . . shy', 'Hurl . . . along', 'scarce . . . by.' All are functional ('not a word wasted'), but the elements that tell most are the verb 'Hurl' and the adjective 'dark'. 'Hurl', at the head of the line, creates its emphatic effect of rapid and abruptly strenuous action instantly. 'Dark', on the other hand, might be objected to as being too general, therefore weak: for nothing characterises contemporary verse practice so much as the individual adjective. But the 'dark' has multiple meanings – as against 'Hurl' – which reverberate beyond the stanza. An instant effect combined with impressions that linger is typical of the Byronic rhetoric.

'Dark'. An obvious, quick, lazy adjective to describe immediately the carcass of the dead bull? Yes, and no. 'Dark'. The arena by now may have been in shadow, or partly so? The bull may have been, like most fighting bulls, black? The thrilling but terrible killing may have impressed as a dark deed? Or, and everyone should have noted this, sweat poured out by man or beast in outbursts of energy or agony darkens skin or the hide? On our first hearing we may not notice the alternatives. But in the rapidity of the statement they are not alternatives. The 'dark' is not an *in*tensive ambiguity, but an *ex*tensive release of significances, in their plurality, because of the scope – as well as the purpose, if scope can be separated from purpose – of the composition. And the delicately 'swift' and 'shy' *hurl* the dead 'dark' thing, on its drag, out of the arena, so quickly that it is hardly seen. One understands that the spectators wish to clear their minds of the object. 'The din of tongues' can rise before the next contest. Quite. But the characteristic 'Hurl', and the phrases concerning the 'Four steeds . . . shy' and 'scarce seen in dashing by' play on that 'dark'. The events happen rapidly, an effect is immediate, but the simple word 'dark' is *ex*tensive.

The suffering of the bull, the struggle of the gladiator, the agonies of the Childe, of the Byronic heroes of the Tales. Discussing torture in *The Two Foscari* with Eckermann, Goethe saw clearly that here Byron was 'just in his element... he was always a self-tormentor', suffering was 'his darling theme'. '*Self*-tormentor': this is probably a pointer to something nearer the truth than the wilful showmanship suggested by 'the pageant of his bleeding heart' or Eliot's 'groomed himself for the rôle of travelling tragedian'. Byron was subjected to early Calvinist influence; he may have been deeply wronged, but he was not entirely guiltless; he may obscurely have wished himself to be wronged, and deeply – and he was guilty of others' hurts if he had so wished to think he was. Like many, he had an impulse towards self-punishment. This is a grim subject, but central to an understanding of Byron. Christians, Calvinists included – a quarter or a fifth of the population of the world – profess, if they understand it, that everyone deserved death for disobedience in eating a fruit. And Byron was prophetic. If the British have exchanged Christianity for an agnostic humanism, they now insist on feeling guilty for their history, for that empire they once had.

The Byronic hero of the Tales drew on his creator's sense of guilt as if it were an abundant capital, and made of infamy a darkly lustrous thing. But the poet was 'more sinned against than sinning'. To complain about being wronged can lead to the charge of self-pity, which is undignified. Indignation even if justified is hardly noble unless it is subsumed by forgiveness – and the woe is related to the woe of others.

In Canto IV he says in the preface, 'I recur from fiction to truth', and Byron speaks in his own person the lines:

> And if my voice break forth, 'tis not that now
> I shrink from what is suffered: let him speak
> Who hath beheld decline upon my brow,
> Or seen my mind's convulsion leave it weak;
> But in this page a record will I seek.
> Not in the air shall these my words disperse,
> Though I be ashes; a far hour shall wreak
> The deep prophetic fulness of this verse,
> And pile on human heads the mountain of my curse!

> That curse shall be Forgiveness. – Have I not –
> Hear me, my mother Earth! behold it, Heaven! –
> Have I not had to wrestle with my lot?
> Have I not suffered things to be forgiven?
> Have I not had my brain seared, my heart riven,
> Hopes sapped, name blighted, Life's life lied away? . . .
>
> But I have lived, and have not lived in vain.
>   (*Childe Harold's Pilgrimage*, IV.
>   cxxxiv–cxxxvii)

Now compare this with the following:

> I am, but what I am, who cares or knows?
> My friends forsake me like a memory lost.
> I am the self-consumer of my woes;
> They rise and vanish, an oblivious host,
> Like shades in love and death's oblivion lost;
> And yet I am, and *live* with shadows tossed
>
> Into the nothingness of scorn and noise,
> Into the living sea of waking dream . . .

That poem by Clare is fine, though one is the more indulgent to the poem through an acquaintance with the biography of the poet. But it is 'Byronic'; it would not have been written but for Byron. Byron provided an example for the other poet to feed on his woe and deliver the touching lament of misery. But there is a difference: Byron fuses – as Clare does not – his misery, or agony, with a contemplation of actualities of agonies and griefs of others outside himself, griefs that must be accepted just as history is accepted. The

> Have I not had my brain seared, my heart riven?
> Hopes sapped, name blighted, Life's life lied away? . . .
>
> But I have lived, and have not lived in vain:

The Poet of Childe Harold

leads into the famous and concretely realised scene of the dying gladiator in the Coliseum of Imperial Rome (cxl–cxli). Byron relates his own woes to those of other men. Like the poet, the gladiator is an exile, separated from his wife and offspring, his fate invoking the 'inhuman shout' of the uncompassionating mob. It was argued, some years ago, that an education in the humanities, if it did not make a man morally better than others, at least gave him a resource denied to others: his training in history or the literatures gave him access to a wide context of collective experience in time and space to which he could refer his personal sufferings. Such a man would at least be spared the vanity of supposing himself a unique victim. Byron had that resource, among others, and draws on it in *Childe Harold* (and vicariously so in *The Prisoner of Chillon* or *The Lament of Tasso*), and it is this more-than-personal spread of grief or melancholy which makes Byron's lament noble or, as Francis Jeffrey said, in his review of Canto IV in 1818, 'majestic' and 'sublime'. And the compassion for men extends beyond them – for things, the ruins of Athens or the ruins of Rome. The beautiful and Byronic poem of John Clare, for all its acute pathos, is not 'noble'; it expresses some self-pity and we respond by sharing it.

Scott and Byron, we remember, were the two poets of vast repute in 1817; Byron accounting Scott the head and summit of Mount Parnassus, and Scott turning to the prose of the Waverley novels when – whatever the other reasons – he felt he was no longer able to compete in rivalry with Byron. There is that amusing passage in Jane Austen's *Persuasion*:

> . . . having talked of poetry, the richness of the present age, and gone through a brief comparison of opinion as to the first-rate poets, trying to ascertain whether *Marmion* or *The Lady of the Lake* were to be preferred, and how ranked *The Giaour* and *The Bride of Abydos*, and moreover how *The Giaour* was to be pronounced, he [Captain Benwick, R. N.] showed himself so intimately acquainted with all the tenderest songs of the one poet, and all the impassioned descriptions of hopeless agony of the other; he repeated, with such tremulous feeling, the various lines which imaged a broken heart, or a mind destroyed by

> wretchedness, . . . that she [Anne] ventured to hope he did not always read only poetry . . .

So Anne recommended a strong dose of prose, the works 'of our best moralists'

> as calculated to rouse and fortify the mind by the highest precepts, and the strongest examples of moral and religious endurances.
>
> (Ch. xi)

Young Captain Benwick had been bereaved of his fiancée, and I dare say there is a danger of sensitive young men over-indulging their emotions by the reading of verse – or by the writing of it – and identifying themselves with the suffering personae of the poets. In which case, I can see, there was more temptation to identify with the Giaour ('however that is to be pronounced') in 1817, or with Childe Harold, than with Mr Prufrock or Gerontion in 1974. Remote from the age and life-style of the prim and timid Mr Prufrock, the present generation finds itself in an age of eloquent violence, 'full of passionate intensity', and active with corsairs and giaours – hijackers, if not 'water-thieves'. These may, or may not, be 'the worst', for not lacking 'all conviction', but their style is Byronic, except that they do not in their actions invariably display the chivalry of the heroes of Byron's Tales. Nevertheless, like those heroes, the new desperadoes are neither timid nor doubting; nor are they less than certain about the value of their political, or other, opinions, or less than proud of the figures they cut. In such a world it would be strange if it could be said that, of the Romantic poets, Byron 'seemed the most nearly remote from the sympathies of every living critic'.

Nearer to readers, and critics, in 1974 than in 1937, Byron would be of more *use* to poets writing today or tomorrow. The poems by Scott and Byron, which so affected Captain Benwick in *Persuasion*, were narrative poems. In the telling of a story, verse can do things which prose cannot do, irrespective of the current health or decline of the novel, and the advantage of verse extends beyond concentration to include the choice of actions – in Arnold's sense of the term, and to Arnold all-important – outside the range and control of prose. Byron, as a master of the narrative poem, offers himself as an exemplar of a *genre* long-neglected but one most likely to render, and interpret, contemporary experience.

I share the view that *Don Juan*, the one great comic poem in our language, is possibly the supreme achievement. But my concern has been mainly with *Childe Harold*, scarcely less great, no less honest, in its own kind, and a necessary stage in the development; for a capacity to develop – or simply to change – is, we recollect, one of the qualities of the major poet.

For *Childe Harold's Pilgrimage* was written from a tragic cast of mind. The comic possibilities of *ottava rima* had still to be discovered; so had the sometimes droll status of *cavalier servente* and the possessive devotion of Teresa Guiccoli. The beyond-the-tragic mood of the lines,

> I would to Heaven that I were so much clay
> As I am blood, bone, marrow, passion, feeling –
> Because at least the past were passed away,
> And for the future – (but I write this reeling,
> Having got drunk exceedingly to-day,
> So that I seem to stand upon the ceiling)
> I say – the future is a serious matter –
> And so – for God's sake – hock and soda-water,

had not yet been reached.

4 THE BYRONIC BYRON

Gilbert Phelps

The term 'the Byronic Byron' is perhaps a paradox for an essay which is based on the belief that there is only one Byron. But it does express that part of his poetic output which has often, in recent years, been shovelled aside as no longer worth serious consideration, and as if it had only the most tenuous connection with *Don Juan* and those poems like *Beppo* or *The Vision of Judgment* which can in some sort be considered pendants to it. No one nowadays is likely to quarrel with the verdict that *Don Juan* represents the peak of Byron's poetic achievement or, if it comes to that, to deny that many of the stanzas of the Byronic Byron are, as Swinburne said (in his 'second thoughts' on the subject) 'blundering, floundering, lumbering and stumbling'.

At the same time one cannot dodge the fact that it was the poetry of the Byronic Byron that seemed most characteristic to his contemporaries and made the first powerful impact both at home and abroad. There is that famous pronouncement of Goethe: 'The English may think of Byron as they please, but this is certain, that they show no poet who is to be compared with him'; and surely it is not sufficient to dismiss this and other similar judgements by European critics on the grounds that they only read Byron in translation – with the usual corollary that it was the very 'badness' of the poetry that made it easy to translate. Neither will it do to argue that these opinions proceeded purely from the emotional and political climate of the day, for many of them, especially those of Goethe, are notably level-headed and primarily aesthetic. In addition there were plenty of enthusiastic responses from Byron's fellow-countrymen, from Jeffrey and Scott to Shelley, which cannot altogether be attributed to local and transient Romantic fashions. The contemporary judgements on this part of Byron's work, in fact, unless we are to assume that those who made them were more than normally naïve and short-sighted, justify one in wondering whether the violence of the reaction against the Byronic Byron doesn't also constitute a paradox that needs explaining.

The suggestion made in this essay, at any rate, is that the recent tendency to split Byron into two very unequal parts and to throw the emphasis almost exclusively on *Don Juan*, has resulted in a lack of balance that fails to do justice to the poetry of the Byronic Byron, and, perhaps, by underestimating the kind of poetic task Byron had set himself, to *Don Juan*, too, as its culmination.

Fundamentally that task (setting aside the purely personal motives which, admittedly, sometimes distort Byron's purpose) was no less than to come to terms, by means of form, symbol, language and imagery, with the contradictory elements in Romanticism, to reconcile its fantastic and unrealisable aspirations with the realities both of the contemporary situation and of the human condition in general.

It might be argued that this in essence was what all the great Romantic poets were, in their varying ways, trying to do. But the peculiar circumstances of Byron's heredity, upbringing, temperament, and life story, blending as they did, and in a manner which he himself not surprisingly often regarded as uncanny, with the whole Romantic *zeitgeist*, made the task his in a unique sense — and in a public as well as a private sphere.

The magnitude and complexity of the task, and of Byron's personal destiny in relation to it, has not been given sufficient weight in assessing the literary quality of his earlier work. In a very real way Byron's 'pilgrimage' was a linguistic one of extraordinary difficulty, a continuous search for a style, a tone of voice, a form, and a dominant group of images that would encompass the welter of conflicting and shifting ideas and impulses with which he had to deal. The idea that he didn't really care about technical matters is contradicted time after time by the correspondence and other sources, almost from the outset of his career. There was, for one thing, his passionate interest in the eighteenth century. Because circumstances, destiny, or his own will (and it is notoriously difficult to disentangle them) had cast him for a public role, as Romantic mouthpiece, scapegoat and ultimately martyr, it was, of course, hardly surprising, that he should have turned for guidance to an age when public utterance was the literary norm. The content of the Byronic Byron may indeed be typically Romantic, but the method, or at any rate the approach, is in many ways typical Augustan rhetoric. Throughout, Byron is a public performer, declaiming on a public platform and always aware of his audience in a way the typical Romantics seldom were. The attributes of the Byronic Heroes, too, are for the most part projected in the generalised terms of Augustan rhetoric. Even the confessional element, which seems on the face of it so characteristically Romantic, is largely cast in the same conventions. In spite of all his complaining and breast-beating, and all the Romantically dark hints, Byron doesn't really probe into his experiences in the way that Wordsworth or Coleridge or Keats did. Rather he was conducting a public demonstration or actor's performance of his 'case' – and this no doubt was one of the reasons why he denied that Childe Harold or any of the other Byronic Heroes were self-portraits: he was right in the sense that they were public projections of a public self. Much of what has been condemned as posturing, in fact, derived from the attempt to utilise the Augustan rhetorical tradition in its more baroque manifestations.

It is yet another of the Byronic paradoxes that the poet who has so often been accused of slap-dash methods of composition was acutely, indeed poignantly, aware that rhetoric to be successful must be subject to precision and control. As early as 1807, while he was still at Cambridge, he wrote on the fly-leaf of his copy of Owen Ruffhead's *The Life of Alexander Pope*:

> Of Pope's pithy conciseness of style Swift – no diffuse writer himself – has so emphatically said:
> > For Pope can in one couplet fix
> > More sense than I can do in six.

It was Pope's ability to match language and emotional content in a public mode that Byron above all admired – and envied. In the comments to Murray in a well-known letter of 1821 on the famous passage from Pope's *Epistle to Dr. Arbuthnot* beginning, 'Let Sporus tremble . . .', to take the most obvious example, Byron demands (after carefully listing the various images): 'Now is there a line of all the passage without the most *forcible* imagery (for his purpose)? Look at the *variety*, at the poetry of the passage – at the *imagination*.' And in another well-known letter (in 1817) he had told Murray that in rereading the eighteenth-century classics, 'particularly Pope', he was 'really astonished . . . at the ineffable distance in point of sense, harmony, effect, and even *Imagination*, passion, and *Invention* between the little Queen Anne's man, and us of the Lower Empire'.

Byron's preoccupation with the eighteenth century was not, of course, only a matter of style. It involved many other factors, including his old-fashioned ideals about aristocracy and *noblesse oblige* (existing side by side with his radicalism); his robust common sense (in spite of all the Romantic posturings); his partial faith in Reason as the only possible counterweight to a metaphysical despair; his genuine concern for a healthy and balanced society; and his equally genuine preference for eighteenth-century modes of thought and feeling – as, for example, in his animadversions on ruin and decay in Canto IV of *Childe Harold*, so reminiscent in tone both of Gibbon and of the Johnson of *The Vanity of Human Wishes*.

As we know, however, Byron did make determined efforts to model himself stylistically on Pope and other eighteenth-century writers. It could, indeed, be argued that here, too, he succeeded better than is usually acknowledged. Leslie A. Marchand, for example, believes that in writing *English Bards, and Scotch Reviewers*, 'Byron's originality and wit sometimes transcended the limitations of the model . . . Echoing the current critical views of Wordsworth, he equalled his master Pope in voicing "What oft was thought, but ne'er so well expressed" – and as illustration Marchand quotes the decidedly pithy and concise lines:

> The simple Wordsworth . . .
> Who, both by precept and example, shows
> That prose is verse, and verse is merely prose.

Byron's lyrics in the Augustan mode, too, often transcend their models, though here the ruling spirit is that of Dryden rather than that of Pope (and W. W. Robson has also pointed out the close affinities between Byron and Rochester). *There Be None of Beauty's Daughters*, for instance, has what Herbert Read called 'an explicit felicity' of the Augustan or Restoration type, and a way of deliberately using 'the obvious cliché to telling effect' – though for 'cliché' one could justifiably substitute 'Augustan generalisation, epithet and personification'. Incidentally, Robson has drawn attention to the sure poetic instinct, and corresponding technical skill, which led Byron to practise 'subtle abrogations of regularity', as in the second line of the same poem:

> There be none of Beauty's daughters
> With a magic like thee.

('Everything is lost', Robson says, 'if we make the semantically insignificant change to "With a magic like *to* thee"'.)

There is, in fact, sufficient evidence to argue not only that Byron was aware of the need for an Augustan precision and control, but also that he was perfectly capable on occasion of exercising them. But the whole point was that, however much he might admire and yearn after eighteenth-century methods, these were no longer adequate for the extraordinarily wide range of content which, owing to the peculiar circumstances which turned him into the Romantic symbol *par excellence*, he had to grapple with – and indeed his qualifying parenthesis '*for his purpose*' [my italics] in his praise of Pope's kind of excellence in the 1821 letter quoted above, indicates that he realised this quite clearly himself.

If, however, the methods evolved by the Augustans to meet the needs of an entirely different world were no longer available to him, neither were those of the typically Romantic poets among his contemporaries. Much of his praise of the former was by way of criticising the latter, and his strictures on Wordsworth, Coleridge, Keats and so on should not entirely be set down to partisanship, limitations of taste, or to the fact that the later Romantics had not yet fully established themselves. When Byron argued that they were 'on the wrong track' he was not only thinking of the condition of English poetry in general, but also of his own dilemma in particular as a man and a poet who had to act out the Romantic *zeitgeist* in public, and at the same time give the performance significance and reality. It was the weaknesses of the Romantics he saw rather than their strength, but these weaknesses were highly relevant from his own point of view, and his exposure of them, moreover, contained a modicum of truth. There really were 'fantastic fopperies' and 'milk and water poetry' in the early Keats – and they were still present in the 1820 volume. Similarly, phrases like 'the Onanism of poetry' and 'mental masturbation' were not so far off the mark in describing Keats's more over-indulgent moments. Byron failed to realise that Keats, too, was struggling to find a language, and that his sensuous excesses were symptomatic of that struggle. He failed to realise, as well, that in poems like the great *Ode to a Nightingale*, Keats was confronting, firmly and triumphantly, the falsities and deceptions of Romanticism, was in a sense as much of an anti-Romantic as he himself – though in fairness to Byron we must remember that after Keats's death he publicly acknowledged that it was 'indignation at Mr Keats's depreciations of Pope' that made him fail 'to do justice to his own genius'. But the point here is that Byron was right in realising that the typical Romantic approaches contained the very dangers of imprecision and indulgence in ingrown fantasy which he had to avoid if he was to fulfil his public role.

Byron's truly daunting dilemma, then, was that neither of the two literary modes open to him suited his case. It was a dilemma that frequently brought him close to despair. He was not, as we know, complacent about his own poetic achievement. As it was to the nineteenth century he belonged and not the eighteenth, he was inevitably forced to approximate to its prevailing idiom in some degree, but as John Addington Symonds put it (in his 1880 essay on Byron), it was for the most part 'a contemptuous compliance with a fashion which the author only tolerated'. His dissatisfaction with his own verse was almost invariably directed against those elements which, in the Romantic decline, were to lead English poetry deeper and deeper into linguistic vagueness, and farther and farther away from contemporary realities. He tempered his pleasure in the publication of the third Canto of *Childe Harold* and Tom Moore's enthusiastic response to it, for example, with the ironic words, '... it is a fine *indistinct* piece of poetical desolation' (my italics). His distrust of 'pure invention', which he described in a letter to Murray (also in 1816) as 'but the talent of a liar', sprang from the same instinct. At times, indeed, he doubted whether poetry – or at any rate the poetic currency of the day – could serve his purpose at all. Hence his several abortive attempts at fiction: as he put it himself in *Beppo*:

> I've half a mind to tumble down to prose,
> But verse is more in fashion – so here goes!

Hence, too, in the letter which he wrote to Tom Moore after a young American had visited him in Ravenna, expecting to meet 'a misanthropical gentleman, in wolf-skin breeches, and answering in fierce monosyllables', his half-comic, half-serious comments: 'I can never get people to understand that poetry is the expression of *excited passion*, and that there is no such thing as a life of passion any more than a continuous earthquake, or an eternal fever. Besides, who would ever *shave* themselves in such a state?' There was also the youthful declaration to his half-sister that he regarded poetry as 'the lava of the imagination whose eruption prevents an earthquake ... I prefer the talents of action – of war, or the senate, or even science, – to all the speculations of those mere dreamers.' And the suspicion that action of some sort was his proper vocation rather than literature increased as he grew older.

This was one of the cruxes of the matter as far as Byron was concerned. The peculiar circumstances of his 'destiny' (as it is impossible to say with any certainty whether it was something that fastened on him, or which he himself, for various complicated psychological reasons, sought out himself, it is perhaps safer to put the word in inverted commas) *did* mean that his creative role could not be a purely literary one. It was this aspect of Byron's poetic task that Matthew Arnold had in mind when he pointed out that as

Byron was 'unfitted' for the prevailing politics of the day (including those of the cautious Whigs) he 'threw himself upon poetry as his organ' (much as Russian writers were obliged to do), and that therefore his 'topics' could hardly be such typically Romantic ones as Queen Mab or the Sensitive Plant, but rather 'the upholders of the old order, George the Third and Lord Castlereagh and the Duke of Wellington', whom he saw as 'the canters and tramplers of the great world'.

It is important to remember that Byron often applied the term 'cant' both to Romantic poetry and to contemporary politics. For example, in his letter to Murray at the time of the Pope controversy he wrote: 'The truth is that in these days the grand *primum mobile* of England is *cant*; cant political, cant poetical, cant religious, cant moral; but always *cant*, multiplied through all the varieties of life. It is the fashion . . . ' The juxtaposition of 'cant political' and 'cant poetical' was not merely related to the fact that some of the Romantic poets, and notably Wordsworth and Southey, had become, in Byron's view, political apostates, but also to his realisation that the dangers of imprecision in language and therefore of the thought and feeling behind it (which were inherent in the Romantic mode) implied a gradually widening breach between poetry and the political and social realities of the world outside. When we recall what happened to much of English Romantic poetry in the Victorian period, with its linguistic decline and increasing withdrawal into private fantasy or into a never-never land of outworn Romantic symbol and convention, so that it was for the most part left to the prose writers to cope with the realities of the society to which they belonged (though it should be added that Keats, the idol of the later Romantics, had in fact shared Byron's perceptions in this respect, as he showed in the revised *Hyperion* – 'The poet and the dreamer are distinct . . . – and in many of his letters), it can be seen that Byron was fundamentally right. From this point of view, in fact, *Don Juan* might be regarded as performing the momentous service of an 'awful warning' against all the varieties of cant and all their implications.

But that 'versified Aurora Borealis' was not produced in a

vacuum, and it was not merely the result of Byron's accidental discovery of *ottava rima*. It was the climax of a linguistic and poetic struggle that had been going on practically from the outset of Byron's career, and the Byronic Byron contained the ingredients, discarded experiments, and stepping-stones that led up to it. For this reason alone the earlier poetry deserves more consideration than it normally receives – especially in view of the fact that the Byronic Byron is very much present in *Don Juan*, performing a vital function of ironic reference and contrast.

Moreover, faced with his linguistic and stylistic dilemma the Byronic Byron did not, in fact, passively 'make do' with the prevailing Romantic modes. On the contrary, he set out to devise what was in effect a poetic discourse of his own. Oddly enough it was Lady Byron who seems to have seen this most clearly, when she declared (after the publication of the third Canto of *Childe Harold*) that her separated husband was 'the absolute Monarch of words, and uses them, as Bonaparte did lives, for conquest, without more regard to their intrinsic value'. Goethe was thinking along the same lines when he wrote that Byron 'spares his language as little as he spares humanity'. Other contemporaries also realised that Byron was attempting something new and unusual. Francis Jeffrey, for instance, in reviewing the first two Cantos of *Childe Harold* in the *Edinburgh Review*, pointed to their 'singular freedom and boldness' as their 'chief excellence', and to 'a tone of self-willed independence and originality about the whole composition'. But on the whole, and especially in recent years, the boldness and originality have been overlooked.

The attempt, in the absence of a supporting tradition which he could share with his public, to impose his will on his materials, to create his own conventions out of his personality and experience, certainly encouraged Byron's tendencies to self-advertisement and, perhaps, to over-hasty composition as he tried out and discarded one 'voice' after another, until he could proclaim triumphantly to Murray that in *Don Juan* he was writing poetry entirely free of 'worn-out machinery'. Nevertheless, if we are to do justice to the poetry of the Byronic Byron this whole process should be taken into account, for Byron is one of those very rare cases in which the ordinary canons of literary criticism are not really applicable. And if one does approach the earlier poetry with the whole process and all the special circumstances in mind, *is* it always as bad as most modern critics suppose?

It is true that the form of poetic discourse which Byron adopted does not as a rule lend itself to detailed verbal analysis. The sharp decline in its reputation (and the hiving off of *Don Juan* and the satirical poems) can be dated to the latter part of the nineteenth century, with its preoccupation with 'pure art' and 'craftsmanship'. It was John Addington Symonds, for example, who in his 1880 essay said that most of Byron's poetry is 'too primitive, too like the raw material of poetry, in its crudity and inequality, to suit our Neo-Alexandrian taste', and that we must admire its author 'for the sweep and strength of his genius or not at all'.

No one would deny that detailed analysis is essential in the assessment of any work of art – generally speaking. But as in all human generalisations there are exceptions, however rare. There are cases where a wide-angled lens is demanded, rather than a close focus. The analysis of texture will reveal obvious flaws, but in some instances a long stretch of material has to be examined, and the coarseness of the weave does not always and necessarily mean weakness in the fabric as a whole. There are some painters, composers, novelists, who must be judged by their broad effects and their extended themes – and there are a few poets, of whom Byron is the prime example.

That is why Byron cannot be adequately represented by selection or quotation (and in fact this is just as applicable to *Don Juan* as it is to the earlier poetry). As Swinburne said (in his earlier and wholly favourable essay) this is poetry that 'can only be judged and appreciated in the mass; the greatness of his work was his whole work taken together'. If that is accepted, it can be seen that most of the themes, images and other elements of great poetry are present, but scattered over a vast area. As with some Elizabethan pastorals, the poetic knot is teased out at interminable length, but encompasses its purpose none the less.

What in essence Byron did, in compensating for the absence of conventions that would serve his purpose by drawing on his own resources, was to substitute energy for conciseness and concentration. This is something different from the inherent vigour possessed by all good poetry. It is the very principle of Byron's creative effort. At bottom it involves both his politics and his personal philosophy, but keeping for the moment to the technical aspects, it is instructive to recall his attack on 'descriptive poetry' as 'the lowest development of the arts'. At first sight this seems surprising, coming from a poet who wrote so much about places, and who has so often been dismissed as a kind of 'verse Baedeker'. But we only have to turn to some of Byron's set-pieces – to the descriptions of Lake Leman, say, in the third Canto of *Childe Harold*, and of Venice, Florence, or Rome in the fourth Canto – to realise that they have no resemblance to descriptive or genre painting. They are the very opposite of 'still life' for the simple reason that they are never 'still', but are, on the contrary, continually thrown into violent agitation by the poet's comments, reflections, moods and personality, and by the restless syntax and punctuation used to convey them. By the same token, the 'Wordsworthian' passages in the third Canto of *Childe Harold* are not at all like Wordsworth in tone and feeling; the invocations of mountain or sky offer no real rest or healing; they are the reflections of, or sometimes the contrasts to, the world of thinking, feeling, suffering and acting men – in a sense Byron never abandoned Pope's edict that 'the proper study of mankind is man', but man thrown into the Romantic wilderness was obviously a very different matter from man contained within a stable and confident society.

It is also important to bear in mind Byron's revealing remark in one of his letters to Murray: 'If I miss my first spring I go growling back to my jungle.' It was an approach not so very different from that of D. H. Lawrence who also, if he considered that he had failed in the first draft of novel or poem, usually set it aside and began all over again, rather than attempting to recast or remould, in the conviction that in this way he would not be interfering with the spontaneous flow of his imagination and emotions. In Lawrence's case, too, it does not always do to judge by passages taken in isolation.

Again, this means that Byron must be read in long stretches.

Only then does the energy establish itself as a genuine creative dynamic; only then do the broad recurrent themes and images fall into place. As Scott so rightly observed, the poetry of the Byronic Byron 'is like the oratory which hurries the hearers along without permitting them to pause on its solecisms and singularities'. Scott also seems to have been the first to compare Byron's poetry to a stream, 'which in its earlier courses bounds over cataracts and rages through narrow and rocky defiles'. It is a helpful image, for just as a stream carries along in its headlong course all kinds of boulders and rocks and pebbles, as well as mud and silt, so the impetus of Byron's verse often carries along the cruder elements, with the result that the *movement* becomes more important than the separate components and often itself constitutes the real 'meaning'.

Scott was also responsible, though, for the most telling and perceptive analogy between *Childe Harold* and certain types of music. Discussing the 'license' Byron had taken with the Spenserian stanza, and the 'harsh' effects that sometimes result, he suggested that 'the effect of the general harmony is, as in music, improved by the judicious introduction of discords wherewith it is contrasted'. He disagreed, in consequence, with 'those who state this occasional harshness as an objection to Lord Byron's poetry', pointing out that when the verse 'labours' it is usually 'in passages where the sense is correspondent to these laborious movements'. Perhaps Byron succeeded in the Augustan ideal of matching sound and sense, within a Romantic context, better than he himself realised — and certainly the only way to appreciate *Childe Harold* is to 'listen' to it as a whole, in order to become aware of its essentially symphonic structure.

'Listening', indeed, must be an important part of one's approach to the Byronic Byron. It is obviously of direct relevance in connection with Byron's public role as orator of the Romantic Movement. It is not easy for the modern reader to respond here. Rhetoric is a mode which, though common in the poetry of the Augustans and their predecessors, has now practically disappeared from English verse. Poetry in other parts of the world, on the other hand, still possesses strong rhetorical traditions — as anyone will know who has attended an international gathering of poets reading their verses in their own tongues – and this, no doubt, is one of the reasons why foreign readers and critics have often been able to appreciate the Byronic Byron more readily than his fellow-countrymen. Never the less, when a determined effort is made to adapt oneself to Byron's rhetorical styles, it becomes apparent, if one listens long enough, that many of the most irritating defects have been caught up in the sweep and urgency of the declamation, and that many of them can be taken as the verbal equivalents of the orator's or actor's gestures, flourishes and grimaces. Byron's poetry is very much an 'acted' poetry, with his speaking voice, or, rather, voices (there are three of them, after all, in *Childe Harold* – the Childe's, a narrator's, and Byron's own) thrown this way and that, almost like those of a ventriloquist.

Byron's concern with the speaking voice is particularly evident in *Childe Harold*. As Paul West has pointed out, the choice of the Spenserian stanza was in many respects an unfortunate one: although Byron would have written a *Childe Harold* anyway, 'with a different stanza he would have written less fustian', for whereas it was perfectly suited to Spenser's slow unfolding of a timeless theme, it was obviously the wrong one for the Byronic Byron. What is interesting, though, is the way in which Byron sought to minimise the difficulties, by breaking up the Spenserian line and rhythm with dashes, commas, italics and all kinds of syntactical devices – almost as if they were 'notations' for the speaking voice.

'Speaking' is not quite the right word, though. It is all too fast for the normal voice. Byron *could* achieve the kind of rounded rhetorical eloquence we find in Pope's *Eloisa to Abelard* – the famous Waterloo stanzas in Canto III of *Childe Harold* at times come close to it – but for the most part his rhetoric is deliberately speeded up, so that the pitch is slightly raised. The speed was vital in order to keep the disparate and largely unformed elements, which would have been too clogging if they had been allowed to settle, in constant motion.

At the same time, the very rapidity of the movement frequently generates heat and light, even in the first two Cantos of *Childe Harold*, full though they are of youthful silliness and, naturally enough, possessing little of the depth and solidity of the later Cantos. There are, for example, the descriptions of Cintra, of Spain, of 'Andalusia's maids', of the bullfight, and of the landscapes and monuments of Ancient Greece, which have a vibrating (and, therefore, still active) brilliance, as if viewed through a heat haze. Such passages, to quote Marchand's telling comment, 'glow with a fervour that lifts them above their own commonplace phrasing'. With the Byronic Byron the combustion is usually what matters most, rather than the materials that went to fuel it.

As a rule it is only when the exigencies of a specific story line demand it that there is a momentary, and often hardly perceptible, slowing down. It is noticeable that in these instances, because they were a necessary part of Byron's overall purpose, the separate elements *are* more carefully moulded, and the Byronic energy becomes perfectly well modulated and controlled. Even in a poem like *The Prisoner of Chillon*, where the characters are chained in a dungeon, Byron displays the remarkable narrative gift of keeping his story at one and the same time concrete, sensuous and mobile. Here and in the other narrative poems, the passages of semi-philosophical reflection are always supported by particularised images and definite references. There is the passage in *The Giaour*, for example (to quote with all the provisos in mind), where the hero reflects on his lost love:

> Yes, Love indeed is light from heaven;
> A spark from that immortal fire
> With angels shared, by Alla given,
> To lift from earth our low desire.
> Devotion wafts the mind above,
> But Heaven itself descends in love;
> A feeling from the Godhead caught,
> To wean from self each sordid thought;
> A Ray of him who form'd the whole;
> A Glory circling round the soul!

And this is immediately followed by a concrete personal comment:

> I grant *my* love imperfect, all
> That mortals by the name miscall . . .

Similarly, the emotions and sensations of the characters are never given in isolation, but are vitally absorbed into the plot and the movement of the verse. Those of Mazeppa, to take another obvious instance, are conveyed in such a way that we never for a moment forget the frantic galloping of the wild horse to which he is strapped:

> The wood was past; 'twas more than noon,
> But chill the air, although in June;
> Or it might be my veins ran cold –
> Prolong'd endurance tames the bold;
> And I was then not what I seem,
> But headlong as a wintry stream,
> And wore my feelings out before
> I well could count their causes o'er . . .

Narrative poetry may have its limitations, and it is out of fashion nowadays. But surely these supple and vigorous lines justify Matthew Arnold's verdict that Byron possessed 'a wonderful power of vividly conceiving a single incident; of throwing himself upon it, of grasping it as if it were real and he saw it, and of making us see and feel it too'.

There is, however, another element in the lines quoted above. Those from *The Giaour* refer to the imperfections of love, and those from *Mazeppa* to emotions and capacities for feeling prematurely exhausted. These are themes which recur constantly, of course, in Byron's verse as well as in his correspondence, journals and autobiographical fragments, and they lead us again into the whole question of the intimate relationship between Byron's personal life and the Romantic Movement as a whole, a relationship which must obviously be understood if the poetry of the Byronic Byron is to be properly appreciated.

The facts of his life story are so intrusive that they tend to obscure the fact that from them emerged a coherent and developing vision of human life and destiny, so that from this point of view Byron's poetic career must be seen as a pilgrimage in search of the forms and symbols that would best express it. In its essentials this philosophy originated in the fascination which the story of the Fall and the expulsion from the Garden of Eden exercised over him as a child, reinforced by the doctrine of Original Sin imbibed from his Calvinist nurse, May Gray, and charged with a special emotional potency because it was she who had prematurely introduced him to sexual experience. The Bible myth became for Byron, in consequence, a particularly apt parable for his own imagined expulsion from an Eden of innocence and security.

Byron's endemic bitterness and disillusionment, his strong feeling that his potentialities for love and happiness had been laid waste, seem to have led him to a singularly bleak interpretation of the ideas of Original Sin; for whereas in Calvinist theology there is a place for a God who knows what he is doing, and who has some concern for mankind, Byron apparently does not admit even that modicum of comfort. As Robert F. Gleckner says in his aptly titled *Byron and the Ruins of Paradise*, Byron's gradually deepening conviction was that 'Man's Fall . . . and his consequent expulsion from Eden is not totally understandable in terms of sin, the commission of some forbidden act; rather, for Byron, man's fall is the providential act of a God who punishes as evidence of his love.' What is more, for Byron the human condition consists of a whole series of expulsions from Eden as man's high aspirations and ideals continually and inevitably crumble into the welter of a chaotic and indifferent universe, itself subject to continual acts of creation and destruction.

It is, naturally, to the more metaphysical poems and dramas that we would need to turn in order to explore Byron's conscious grappling with these ideas. To *Prometheus*, for example, whose Titan, endlessly punished for the crime of love, and a 'sign' of man's 'funereal destiny', was a particularly apt symbol for Byron. To *Manfred*, with its hero 'half dust, half deity', hounded not so much by the moral guilt of an actual sin as by the guilt, as M. K. Joseph has said, of being 'a member of the human race'. Above all, perhaps, to *Cain*, which occupies a special position in that it deals directly with the lost Eden myth – and also perhaps because Goethe wrote of its 'burning spiritual vision' which 'penetrates beyond all comprehension into the past and the present', while both Scott and Shelley compared it to Milton's *Paradise Lost*. It would also be necessary to examine that unaccountably neglected poem, *Darkness*, with its terrifying picture of a world dying as the result of some cosmic cataclysm, in the course of which all human values have been destroyed and man has reverted to a kind of Hobbesian savagery – such a world as one might envisage 'after the Bomb'.

But here the general point to be stressed is that because Byron's philosophy (to use the grand term for the sake of convenience), bleak and forbidding though it may be, runs through the whole of his work, from the earliest poems with their constant references to a childhood Eden that can be momentarily recaptured through memory, only to be destroyed by contact with the reality of the present, right up to *Don Juan* with its bitter vision of mankind as merely 'maggots of some huge Earth's burial', relieved only by momentary gleams of the lost ideal (as in the Haidée interlude or in the 'Isles of Greece' stanzas) which are bound by their very nature to be transitory – his poetry is much more consistent and through-grained than is generally recognised. When once this fact is given its proper due, the earlier poems take on unexpected vibrations and reveal new depths and subtleties.

To take another example from the narrative poems – in *The Prisoner of Chillon* it is usually assumed that the theme is simply the typical Romantic one of man's defiant faith in liberty; it is that, of course, but its fundamental concern is the eternal condition of man (as Byron saw it), imprisoned by his mortality, his darkness relieved only by occasional and illusory rays of light. In other words, it is a more serious poem than conventional criticism has allowed.

Or take an even more hackneyed example – *The Destruction of Sennacherib*. This belongs to *Hebrew Melodies* – and it is worth remarking that Byron would naturally have been interested in 'Israel's scatter'd race', forced to 'wander witheringly' (as he says in *The Wild Gazelle*) as powerful symbols of the universal condition of Byronic man, and most of the poems in the collection are either laments, hymns to the loss, by one means or the other, of love and beauty, or celebrations of destruction.

In *Sennacherib* the intrusive drum beat (combined with the fact that it has for so long been an anthology favourite) usually results in over-hasty reading. It is in fact a much deeper and more subtle poem than the first hypnotic gallop through would suggest. It is for one thing curiously ambivalent in its attitudes and in the responses it invites. The stirring rhythms induce the sensation of being caught up in the Assyrian army, charging with them to glorious victory – but this of course is dead against the moral and religious drift, for the Assyrians are the enemies of the Lord, and we should be on *his* side, not theirs. Then again, most of the beauty, colour, brightness, life – the 'purple and gold', the 'sheen of their spears', the 'green' of the summer forest, and so on – are associated with the 'bad' Assyrians; and they are quickly swallowed up in images of horror and destruction – 'wither'd and strown'; 'the eyes of the sleepers wax'd deadly and chill'; 'cold as the spray of the rock-beating surf' – all of them the work of the Lord. The contrast between the stir of pride and vitality represented by the Assyrians, and the dead and desolate landscape achieved by the Lord, together with the tug between our imaginative sympathies and our conventional reactions, creates, in other words, a genuine tension – one which underlies Byron's attitude towards the Almighty throughout his work, and which indirectly involves the whole question of the Satanic side of Romanticism and the 'Romantic Agony'.

The surface movement of the poem is so rapid and dramatic that we are not always aware of these underlying tensions: but they exist in most of the poems of the Byronic Byron. In this limited sense, indeed, they *will* stand up to close analysis far better than most modern critics admit.

Such an analysis, bearing in mind Byron's overall vision, would reveal fresh significances in Byron's characteristic images and strings of imagery. The sea, to take the obvious example, is not *always* used in vague Romantic gestures. It can communicate not only Byron's own chaotic feelings of loss and rejection, but those of suffering humanity in general:

> ... for I am as a weed
> Flung from the rock, on Ocean's foam to sail
> Where'er the surge may sweep, the tempest's breath prevail.

Sea imagery is frequently combined, too, with that of wreckage and destruction, as when in the fourth Canto of *Childe Harold* Byron wonders whether 'from the floating wreck which Ruin leaves behind' he might 'from the planks, far shatter'd o'er the rocks' build for himself 'a little bark of hope', in which he may once more venture:

> To battle with the ocean and the shocks
> Of the loud breakers, and the ceaseless roar
> Which rushes on the solitary shore
> Where all lies founder'd that was ever dear.

And of course *Childe Harold's Pilgrimage* ends with an evocation of the ocean as what M. K. Joseph has called 'the great unchanging, timeless image of change and time'.

Mountains, winds, light, fire, stars and many other characteristic Byronic images all contain the vibrations and ambiguities communicated by the clash between Byron's Romantic aspirations and his bleak philosophical outlook, while threading through the whole of his work is the motif of the Fall, with its related imagery of blighted trees, fruits, flowers and buds.

At the same time, the point made earlier that the Byronic Byron has to be approached with a wide-angled lens is applicable here too. Taken separately the images do not (as the quotations above make clear) produce very distinguished poetry. Similarly in the stanzas describing the battlefield of Waterloo, in Canto III of *Childe Harold*, rhetorical expressions like 'Earthquake's spoil' for the French dead who, like Napoleon's hopes, are 'sepulchred below'; or the 'red rain' of blood that has made 'the harvest grow', strike one at first sight as forced and stale. But within the total image of the battle, which is in turn related to the outcome of the French Revolution as a further example of man's aspirations perpetually doomed to disappointment, to Napoleon as the prototype of a heroic and suffering, but imperfect Prometheus, and thus to Byron's total vision of chaos and anarchy, they play their part and even contribute in their stridency to the general cacophony. The same is true of most of the other metaphors and similes that cluster round other extended images, such as Ancient Greece (often depicted as a lost Golden Age) or the ruins of Rome.

As with the other ingredients of the verse, the individual images are kept in motion, and so related to the main 'stream', by the Byronic energy. At the same time the energy, in this connection too, must be seen as something more than a simple Romantic frenzy when we place it in the context of Byron's cosmic vision. At times it is indeed the energy of despair; but in the light of Byron's assumption that man's hopes of a better world must be eternally frustrated, it is also, by a kind of desperate paradox, an assertion of heroic defiance as the one positive dynamic that is left to mankind. In this sense it can be regarded as analogous to the energy, continually creating in order to destroy, that permeates the universe itself — and another aspect of Byron's 'heroism', therefore, is that in spite of his implacable pessimism he placed himself, so to speak, on the side of creation.

Inevitably this brings us to the most famous of all Byron's extended images — that of the Byronic Hero. It was one of the most potent ever created, and to do it full justice would involve a survey of the whole field of nineteenth-century political and social history, literature, painting, music, architecture and taste. Here only the general point can be made that this, too, is a more complex image than has always been recognised — and one that is also related to Byron's philosophical position. On the political side it was a dual symbol: of protest against tyranny on the one hand (as in the stanzas on Greece in the second Canto of *Childe Harold*) and, on the other, of hopes and aspirations already thwarted, after the brief and illusory promise of the French Revolution. In this connection we need to remind ourselves that the Europe which Byron knew was very different from that of the earlier Romantics, and of the young Wordsworth with his heady cry:

> Bliss was it in that dawn to be alive,
> But to be young was very heaven!

Byron's period, by contrast, was that of the Terror, the rise of Napoleon Bonaparte (the flawed Prometheus), the Napoleonic Wars, the restoration of the *anciens régimes*, and the ruthless reaction and repression that followed it — not to mention the mounting evidence, at least as far as Britain was concerned, that drastic changes in social, economic and human relationships were taking place as the Industrial Revolution gathered momentum. There had, in other words, been a whole series of 'expulsions from Eden', and the process showed every sign of continuing.

Thus the sense of blighted hopes, the disillusionment, melancholy and despair that belonged to Byron's own temperament and life-experience, when transmuted into the poetic creation of the Byronic Hero, expressed more powerfully than any other artistic symbol of the period the political and social malaise of a whole generation. Nothing could be farther from the truth than to regard Childe Harold and the other heroes of the Byronic Byron as the mere products of theatrical melodrama, despite the scowling brows, curling lips, dark cloaks and darker secrets. These crude elements are also thrown into violent motion by the Byronic energy — and however ham the acted performance it was the energy of unappeased furies. It is of particular significance, for example, that the Byronic Hero exercised an especially powerful influence in Russia, the very country where, after the brief promise held out by the Tsar Alexander I's youthful professions of liberal ideas, autocratic repression was at its most thorough and stultifying, especially after the collapse of the Decembrist conspiracy of 1821 (led by young officers who had been with the Russian army of occupation in Paris and had there been fired by the dying embers of the old revolutionary fervour). For proof we only have to turn to some of the characters of Pushkin (who learned English in order to read Byron in the original), to the hero of Lermontov's poem *The Demon*, or to the Pechorin of the latter's novel, *A Hero of Our Own Times*.

In Russia, as the autocracy became increasingly harsh, and every possible political outlet for ardent young spirits was ruthlessly sealed, the Byronic Hero gradually changed into the utterly hopeless, bored and passive 'superfluous man' of later Russian fiction, or into the Satanic kind of character we find in many of Dostoyevsky's novels. It is to Byron's credit that in spite of his own ingrained pessimism he did not allow himself or his heroes (and after his ostracism from England in 1816 he became in effect his own Byronic Hero, a merging that is signalised by the gradual absorption in the later Cantos of *Childe Harold* of the Childe's voice into his own) to take the same course. Side by side with his own personal despair, and the deepening and darkening of his personal philosophy, there was a sharper awareness of the symbolic role that circumstances had thrust upon him, and for the rest of his life he never lost sight of it. Even the fourth Canto of *Childe Harold*, with its sombre evocations of dying empires and the fading glories of human cultural achievement, and of his own situation as 'A ruin amidst ruins', is nevertheless still a political poem, with its defiant cry, against the very current of his own experience and convictions:

> Yet, Freedom! Yet thy banner, torn, but flying,
> Streams like the thunder-storm *against* the wind . . .

(and surely this at least is an instance where the italics are fully justified). Gradually, too, the earlier largely undirected explosions of defiance and energy moved towards a political focus, until eventually the Byronic Hero became a martyr and the Byronic Byron had achieved his final apotheosis.

The fact that in order to become complete the symbol of the Byronic Hero had to spill over from poetry into action should not, however, detract from its literary value and significance. The political passions it expressed, together with the whole crisis of Liberalism, may have receded into the past, like one of Byron's vanished empires, with their illusory gleams of a promised Eden, but its tremendous impact at the time and for many years after proved how powerful it had been, and in itself prompts one to ask whether it could really have been the creation of a poet of inferior genius.

In any case it had a far wider significance than the purely political one. The Byronic Heroes of *Childe Harold* and the verse tales are not only the lost souls of the post-revolutionary reaction. They are the lost souls, too, of the dying Romantic Movement, with its myth of the perfectibility of man, as an uglier and more materialistic world emerged from one that had in some respects, perhaps, been gentler and more civilised – and this no doubt was one of the reasons that prompted Lamartine to describe *Childe Harold* as 'the only epic possible in our day'. In setting himself against a Romantic optimism Byron may, in his personal behaviour, in his moods of satiety and melancholy, and in his onslaughts on his merciless God, have come close at times to the Satanism or diabolism of the Romantic decadence. But somehow he always countered these tendencies, both through action and by means of a desperate stoicism that sought, in the midst of discontinuity, to 'create out of universal death and chaos [to quote Gleckner] a coherent vision of fragments sufficient to sustain man in his dying'.

In addition, the Byronic Byron was also expressing that aspect of Romanticism which stretches back to the Renaissance, to a time when modern man first stepped out from the lost Eden of a secure and unquestioned faith in a merciful God and began his long and lonely pilgrimage into the wilderness of a world 'out of joint' and apparently emptied of transcendental hope. The pilgrimage is, of course, by no means over, and from this point of view Childe Harold and the other Byronic heroes are timeless pilgrims, universal symbols of loss and disorientation. It would even be possible, indeed, to argue that in a sense *Don Juan*, with its man-of-the-world acceptance of a mundane 'reality', and the consequent containment of an energy whose very nature was its perpetual flow, without any bounds at all, was an abrogation of this task.

What, at any rate, is certain is that the Byronic Byron has a continuing and universal relevance. It was no accident, for example, that James Joyce should have introduced Childe Harold, the

Giaour and other Byronic Heroes into *Finnegans Wake*, itself a powerful parable of chaos and disorientation. Joyce clearly saw them, and Childe Harold in particular (who becomes, to all intents and purposes, his 'Everyman'), as prototypes of modern man, wandering exiled and lost in an anarchic universe. The world of the Byronic Byron is that of Joyce, as it is that of the W. B. Yeats who wrote:

> Things fall apart; the centre cannot hold,
> Mere anarchy is loosed upon the world.

Or that of T. S. Eliot who wrote in *The Waste Land*: 'These fragments I have shored against my ruins' – and one of whose characters cries out:

> I can connect
> Nothing with nothing.

Or, indeed, that of Samuel Beckett or Harold Pinter or David Storey or a dozen other modern writers who find themselves obliged to push homelessness and exile to the farthest limits of deprivation and nullity.

The Byronic Byron is still full of meaning to all those writers of our own waste land who struggle to give form and coherence to its apparent fragmentation and meaninglessness – and if *Don Juan* represents the crown of Byron's poetic achievement, it is certainly time that the Byronic Byron had his day.

5 BYRON AND THE SATIRIC TEMPER

P. M. Yarker

One of the many bewildering features of satire is the fact that, although to be effective it must immediately be recognised, it is notoriously difficult to define. So far as it is an art it has form, or forms; but these have been so various that to define them in detail leaves the general nature of satire as elusive as ever. Perhaps it is best approached as a mood or temper, but even here the reference is necessarily wide. Most accounts have placed it between two extremes, traditionally represented by Horace and Juvenal. John Dennis wrote, for example:

> There is in *Horace* almost every where an agreeable Mixture of good Sense, and of true Pleasantry, so that he has every where the principal Qualities of an excellent Comick Poet. And there is almost every where in *Juvenal*, Anger, Indignation, Rage, Disdain, and the violent Emotions and vehement Style of Tragedy.[1]

This still leaves much unsaid, for although satire may incline to either comedy or tragedy, it is different in kind from both. Moreover, Dennis's division is not properly between comedy and tragedy but between a good-humoured, witty mode, and a violent and angry one. Satire has been called the offspring of malice and wit, and these two elements are sufficiently basic to provide a useful clue to its nature. Malice supplies the aggressiveness, the sense of personal injury that gives it motive and energy. Wit supplies everything else: the underlying perceptiveness, the weapons of laughter or disdain, the immunity from retaliation. Both elements are always necessary, for the most savage attack needs wit to distinguish it from mere abuse; and however urbane and detached a comment may be, it still needs a touch of malice to supply a motive.

In his early days, at any rate, Byron firmly believed in the malicious origin of satire:

> Satiric rhyme first sprang from selfish spleen:
> You doubt—see Dryden, Pope, St. Patrick's Dean.
> (*Hints from Horace*, ll. 115–16)

Just as *The Dunciad* began in Pope's fury at Theobald's treatment of his edition of Shakespeare, so *English Bards, and Scotch Reviewers* had its origin in Byron's anger at the review of *Hours of Idleness* in the *Edinburgh Review*, of which he supposed Jeffrey to be the author. Hence his attack on Jeffrey as the 'Scotch Reviewer' in the poem. But *The Dunciad* was from the beginning not merely a retaliation for Theobald's strictures but an attack on bad writing generally. And Byron followed Pope in this also, in his attacks on the 'English Bards'.

At first Byron clearly felt an affinity with the sterner Juvenalian mood, for the opening lines of *English Bards, and Scotch Reviewers* are a paraphrase of those of Juvenal's First Satire, in which he mounts a fleeting attack on the poetasters. Other echoes occur in the first hundred lines or so. Even at the end of the poem Byron represents himself as one, naturally kindly, whom life has rendered callous and vindictive:

> The time hath been, when no harsh sound would fall
> From lips that now may seem imbued with gall;
> Nor fools nor follies tempt me to despise
> The meanest thing that crawl'd beneath my eyes;
> But now, so callous grown, so changed since youth,
> I've learn'd to think, and sternly speak the truth . . .
> (ll. 1053–8)

'Sternly speak the truth' is a reference back to Juvenal; but the whole passage, from a veteran of twenty-one, has an unreal quality suggesting that the poem is not quite what it seems. Byron's presumption in writing it, has often been remarked; but it is important to reflect that he wrote not as himself, nor even (as the passage quoted might suggest) in an impersonation of himself, but as the conscious imitator of others: of Gifford most immediately; but beyond him Pope, and beyond Pope, Dryden and the Roman satirists. In attempting this imitation he not only worked in an idiom that was not his own and did not suit him well, but he also assumed an attitude towards his material that was equally alien. He admired Gifford inordinately, and Pope almost to idolatry. Yet his own tastes were really quite different from either. Gifford was his older contemporary, but how far removed were his affinities from Byron's a casual reading of *The Baviad* and *The Maeviad* will reveal:

>   Now fools and children void their brains by loads
>   And itching grandams spawn lascivious odes;
>   Now lords and Dukes, curs'd with a sickly taste,
>   While Burns' pure healthful nurture runs to waste,
>   Lick up the spittle of a bed-rid muse,
>   And riot in the sweepings of the stews.[2]

This is in the plague tradition, still strongly surviving from the seventeenth century when Pope wrote *The Dunciad*, but noticeably harsh in 1794, when *The Baviad* appeared. Its ratiocination is clear enough; the Della Cruscans, like the Dunces, were an epidemic disease, and a diseased imagery was appropriate. Yet in the interim Dr Johnson had complained that Pope 'had an unnatural delight in ideas physically impure', and a certain squeamishness can be detected in the latter part of the century. Byron produced outrageous images by the score, and filled his verses with innuendo. Nor did he shrink from the full presentation of physical horrors, like the carrion dogs of Corinth, or poor Pedrillo's gruesome end, or the battlefield of Ismail. Yet it is doubtful if anywhere in his poetry will be found so scabrous a line as

>   Lick up the spittle of a bed-rid muse . . .

Certainly not in *English Bards, and Scotch Reviewers*, where the nearest approach to it merely makes a distant reference to vaccination among the catalogue of modern wonders:

> The cow-pox, tractors, galvanism, and gas.

The remark is often made that whereas Gifford and Pope attacked the pigmies of their time, Byron assailed the giants in Scott, Wordsworth, Coleridge, and even Southey, to say nothing of the all-powerful Edinburgh Reviewers. This is true, but it was not merely a matter of audacity. The reason lay in the difference between Pope's position and Byron's. Pope, and Gifford too, felt that they were repelling the onslaught of a swarm of paltry but insidious agents of spiritual disease. The fools and dunces might in themselves be insignificant. But their very triviality became a menace when the critics hailed it as excellence, for then it threatened the foundations of taste. Gifford said of the newspaper the *World*:

> as its conductors were at once ignorant and conceited they took upon themselves to direct the taste of the town, by prefixing a short panegyric to every trifle which came before them.[3]

For similar reasons, the race of the Booksellers is the most circumstantial and debased of all the heroic games that celebrate the enthronement of the King Dunce in *The Dunciad*; and the prize is the magic power to turn dunces into wits. Pope showed Gifford that the licence of fools could threaten the foundations of order.

This seriousness is reflected in the epic scale of *The Dunciad*, which eventually received a full apparatus of the supernatural, and into which Pope introduced elements of the terrible, not wholly spurious. But there is no such firm purpose behind Byron's poem, and no corresponding epic structure. *English Bards* has, at best, only the sort of associative sequence that we find in *Childe Harold*. Its most serious lines suggest a saecular scheme of changing generations, with a decline in standards. There is a glimpse of the fall of Athens and of Rome, a hint that London may soon follow. Briefly the mood approaches that of *Childe Harold*; it nowhere attains the sombre menace of the conclusion of *The Dunciad*. Byron soon turns away to 'themes less lofty', and this is the pattern of the poem as a whole. There is no consistency of purpose behind it, as there is with *The Dunciad* or even Gifford's poems. Byron disclaims any responsibility towards the serious problems of the age, for

> not belong
> To me the arrows of satiric song;
> The royal vices of our age demand
> A keener weapon, and a mightier hand.
> Still there are follies, e'en for me to chase,
> And yield at least amusement in the race;
> Laugh when I laugh, I seek no other fame;
> The cry is up, and scribblers are my game.
>
> (ll. 37-44)

This is not the mood of *The Dunciad*, or of Gifford. It suggests only a *jeu d'esprit*, a piece of virtuosity pursued for the fun of it.

Never the less, Byron was seriously concerned to supply the criticism that he found wanting in 'the nation's censors'; but it was a task in which from the outset he was at a serious disadvantage. In Pope's day the established canons of criticism were understood and accepted. There was general subscription to the doctrine of good sense, and to truths that had merely to be stated to be known and acknowledged. But Byron could not count on such a consensus. Sense and wit were merely 'fabled graces', half-remembered from a distant age. Without such established and universally acknowledged standards Byron had difficulty in submitting to the restriction of the heroic couplet in which Pope had moved with such ease and celerity. He faced a dilemma. Without an acknowledged canon of criticism he must explain the principle of each attack as he makes it, thus appearing laborious and inflated. Or, lacking a sophisticated appeal to good sense, he must attack his victims on grounds of fatuity so absurd as to be self-evident, thus losing wit and incisiveness. He used both methods, with the result that his attacks are generally too loose or too broad. Gifford, who suffered to some extent from the same difficulties, surmounted them by putting the necessary critical explanations into the Notes, which are several times as long as the poems. But Byron, trying to keep as much as possible within the poem itself, found himself cramped, and had to expand to a paragraph what Pope could have expressed, and even emphasised, within a single couplet.

In the lines on Southey, for example, Byron begins with the valid criticism that, whereas formerly the epic was 'The single wonder of a thousand years', latterly such men as Southey had reeled off a new one every year. It was a point which in Pope's day could have stood by itself; but Byron finds it necessary to produce a catalogue of Southey's poems, giving half a dozen lines of explanation to each. He had not yet developed the animosity towards Southey that he later so felicitously exhibited, but he attacked him, nevertheless. The effect, however, was hardly painful:

> Oh, Southey! Southey! cease thy varied song!
> A bard may chant too often and too long:
> As thou art strong in verse, in mercy spare!
> A fourth, alas! were more than we could bear.
> (ll. 225–8)

It is a little too limp and flaccid, too good-natured. In the well known attacks on Wordsworth and Coleridge Byron followed the other course, developing nonsense so palpable that it could not be missed. Thus, Wordsworth is praised as the hero of *The Idiot Boy*, and Coleridge suffers similarly from having written *Lines to a Young Ass*. But the weapon is blunt and harmless.

Closest to the method of *The Dunciad* was the sustained attack on Jeffrey, against whom alone Byron felt the goad of 'selfish spleen'. To mount this attack he made use of a supernatural apparatus, with Caledonia's goddess presiding in place of Pope's Great Anarch, and Jeffrey receiving from Judge Jeffries of the Bloody Assize the ceremonial halter marking his accession to the office of National Hangman. This last image has something of the authentic quality, and the lines presenting it an appropriate crispness:

> Let Jeffries' shade indulge the pious hope,
> And greeting thus, present him with a rope:
> 'Heir to my virtues! man of equal mind!
> Skill'd to condemn as to traduce mankind,

> This cord receive, for thee reserved with care,
> To wield in judgment, and at length to wear.'
>
> (ll. 454–9)

But in the fantasy that follows Byron felt too much had been made of Jeffrey's farcical duel with Moore (much funnier in fact than it appears in the poem). 'All this is bad, because personal', he wrote beside it in 1816.

In the end, of course, they all forgave Byron, or nearly all, and he forgave them – all but Southey, that is. On Jeffrey, in the Postscript added to the second edition of the poem, he made the disarming comment,

> I suppose I must say of Jeffrey as Sir Andrew Aguecheek saith, 'an I had known he was so cunning of fence, I had seen him damned ere I fought him.'[4]

And, in 1816, he wrote:

> The greater part of this satire I most sincerely wish had never been written – not only on account of the injustice of much of the critical, and some of the personal part of it – but the tone and temper are such as I cannot approve.[5]

Such a palinode seems to reduce the whole concept of satire to a mere whim, the reaction to a sudden angry mood to be regretted as soon as it was past. That this was true of Byron at the time there is the testimony of his friend Dallas, who had been his close associate in writing *English Bards*. Dallas wrote: 'His feelings, rather than his judgment, guided his pen,' and the form of the poem bears him out. Discursive, over-emphatic, always expanding and elaborating, it suggests the opposite of the cold malice that calculates the exact force and timing to produce the greatest hurt. Byron seems too amused and excited by the poem to consider its effect on its victims, whom he had no real wish to harm.

But to argue from this that he lacked the spirit of satire would be quite wrong, for there is a further characteristic of satire that

Byron shared to the full. Satire is always equivocal. It attacks the worst of things only through implication of the best. If it ridicules a man it does so because he is less than he should be.

> Who but must laugh if such a man there be?
> Who would not weep if Atticus were he?

Pope's couplet sums up the dual vision with which the satirist views the world. Every satirical portrait implies an ideal one; every assault on the way things are depends upon an understanding that they could be better. Satire springs from the divided self. It is an appeal to our better nature as much as an attack on our worse. The satirist faces a dilemma in which no compromise is possible. He feels, often with passion, the urge to better things; but the effect is to sharpen his awareness of present shortcomings. At one extreme satire is a work of exasperation; its most urgent task is not the punishment of folly and vice but the destruction of complacency. Its true target is not the immediate victim but the wider audience, to sting them from indifference and unjustified optimism. And this is a curiously personal matter. Unable to escape the oppressive sense of life's inadequacy, the satirist feels the comfortable delusion of the satisfied with the smart of personal injury that goads him to retaliate.

Most writers are satirical at times; it is an inevitable response to the human condition. But to some the sense of life's division is so powerful that satire is their natural outlet. They cannot avoid the dual vision, the awareness of the gap between the actual and the ideal, or between the fatuous and the true. This duality is evident, in one form or another, in almost everything Byron wrote.

Sir Egerton Brydges, in his *Letters on the Character and Poetical Genius of Lord Byron* (1824) wrote:

> Some minds are cast in so sombre a mould, that they seem naturally disposed to delight in gloom, mysteries, and terrors. There is something in human existence which dissatisfies them, and produces a discontent and ill humour that drive them to seek familiarity with painful emotions... No one, I think, will deny

that this was the bent and ruling genius of Lord Byron.[6]

What Brydges described in his *Letters* was not the character of Byron himself, of which he knew little, but a composite picture of his earlier heroes. Byron complained many times of this confusion, but he was himself partly to blame for it. For in drawing these characters he took the figure, perennial in literature, of the guilt-haunted, introspective man, and gave it substance and vitality by endowing it with his own experiences and reactions, and informing it with his own conflicting moods. The wide popularity of *Childe Harold* and the Turkish Tales was partly due to the fact that this figure, recently sentimentalised in the man of feeling, or rendered sinister in the Gothic villain, was very familiar to the European consciousness at the turn of the nineteenth century. The mood it exemplified of world-weariness tormented by vestiges of energy and idealism was, for a number of reasons, peculiarly congenial to the times.

Recently it had been given a further dimension by the teaching of Kant, the effect of which was to emphasise the divided self. Kant sharply distinguished between the empirical self of causation and the moral self of autonomy. Living in the world of space and time we cannot escape its laws, the chief of which is that of cause and effect. In this world nothing is free, for everything is governed by its antecedents. Considered thus man must be seen as merely obeying his reflexes, inherited or conditioned. Were he always to follow his inclinations, acting only to secure happiness in the world, he would be entirely unfree, completely subject to the laws of cause and effect. But it is possible to act against our inclinations, and even to feel that, although our antecedents have made us what we are, yet we ought to be different. In this awareness we find the autonomy that Kant saw as the basis of freedom and morality. To act rightly is to act on these disinterested principles. Any action taken to achieve a result in the world is a surrender to the law of causation. In Kant's terms, then, each individual is faced with a conflict between his natural desire for happiness and the awareness that to act in pursuit of it is to forfeit his freedom. This teaching cast doubt on the eighteenth-century belief that happiness is the goal of life. It also provided a means of compensation for those who saw themselves as outcast or oppressed. Amid the humiliations of the world it became important to cultivate the individual integrity. To be oneself, regardless of the demands and conventions of society, was to attain a success far greater than those who, enjoying all the fruits of earthly life, were nevertheless enslaved by its laws. Yet the desire for happiness remained, and what was thus despised as inferior was nevertheless the object of envy and longing.

This division of the self is the stuff of satire. It is a little like Gulliver's homecoming from the land of the Houyhnhnms, when he said,

> My wife and family received me with great surprize and joy, because they had concluded me certainly dead; but I must freely confess, the sight of them filled me only with hatred, disgust, and contempt; and the more, by reflecting on the near alliance I had with them.

Byron, with his Calvinistic childhood, his lameness, his mother's stultifying influence, and even perhaps his immediate ancestry, found it congenial to despise the shallow, obvious values of society. Yet, far from being a recluse, he was one of the most companionable of men, vivacious, gay, affectionate. On receiving Jeffrey's review of Canto III of *Childe Harold* he asked Moore to tell Jeffrey

> what you know, that I was not, and, indeed, am not even *now*, the misanthropical and gloomy gentleman he takes me for, but a facetious companion, well to do with those with whom I am intimate, and as loquacious and laughing as if I were a much cleverer fellow.
>
> (10 March 1817)

'I suppose now', he added, 'I shall never be able to shake off my sables in public imagination.'

But the sables were not wholly superfluous. The first Canto of *Childe Harold* describes quite explicitly the process by which the gay world of the pursuit of happiness is abandoned in a mood of introspection and withdrawal:

> Yet oft-times in his maddest mirthful mood
> Strange pangs would flash across Childe Harold's brow,
> As if the Memory of some deadly feud
> Or disappointed passion lurked below;
> But this none knew, or haply cared to know;
> For his was not that open, artless soul
> That feels relief by bidding sorrow flow,
> Nor sought he friend to counsel or condole,
> Whate'er this grief mote be, which he could not controule.
>
> (I. viii)

This stanza suggests the self-division of Byron's heroes and hints at the reason for it. The next makes clear that although Childe Harold despises his companions as 'heartless parasites' he nevertheless longs for companionship, while at the same time enjoying the dark but exquisite pleasure of being misunderstood. For his pangs are not an intolerable anguish to him. On the contrary, they are the source of perverse and hidden pleasure, to be nursed in secret, and fed with deprivation and self-exile.

This equivocal mood, in which grief is jealously preserved from those who do not share it, is evidence of the satiric temper in Byron's poetry at that time. The appeal of his heroes lay not only in the urge to revolt and assert their individuality. It lay also in the suggestion that failure in the ordinary affairs of life is a fine thing. Those who succeed do so because they are inferior, deficient in some essential sensibility. The revolt was really against the very conditions of existence. Lara, for example, feels himself an alien:

> He stood a stranger in this breathing world,
> An erring spirit from another hurl'd:
> A thing of dark imaginings, that shaped
> By choice the perils he by chance escaped:
> But 'scaped in vain, for in their memory yet
> His mind would half exult and half regret:

> With more capacity for love than earth
> Bestows on most of mortal mould at birth,
> His early dreams of good outstripp'd the truth,
> And troubled manhood follow'd baffled youth,
> With thoughts of years in phantom chase misspent,
> And wasted powers for better purpose lent:
> And fiery passions, that had pour'd their wrath
> In hurried desolation o'er his path,
> And left the better feeling all at strife
> In wild reflection o'er his stormy life;
> But haughty still and loth himself to blame,
> He call'd on Nature's self to share the shame,
> And charged all faults upon the fleshly form
> She gave to clog the soul, and feast the worm . . .
>
> (*Lara*, I, ll. 315–34)

The sense of belonging to two worlds – the one to which he aspires forever beyond his grasp, the other which he despises all too much with him – is basically the attitude of the satirist. Or, more truly perhaps, that of a victim of satire, like Gulliver returning from the land of the Houyhnhnms. But one essential feature is missing. There is bitterness, there is resentment, there is scorn; but no exasperation, no fierce onslaught of personal spleen that turns the whole thing sour. Although Byron repeatedly approaches this mood, or its adjacent one, the sardonic, he does not, in *Childe Harold* or the Tales, quite embrace it. When, for example, he contemplates a skull his mood is entirely elegiac, although satire is but a step away:

> Look on its broken arch, its ruin'd wall,
> Its chambers desolate, and portals foul;
> Yes, this was once ambition's airy hall,
> The dome of thought, the palace of the soul:
> Behold through each lack-lustre, eyeless hole,
> The gay recess of wisdom and of wit,
> And passion's host, that never brook'd control:
> Can all saint, sage, or sophist ever writ,

People this lonely tower, this tenement refit?

(II. vi)

But the avoidance of satire in such a passage is not because the poet consciously draws back. On the contrary, it is not because he says too little but because he has said too much. He loses contact with the object in a flood of generalities and rhetoric. Consequently he does not feel the final urge to punish and destroy, the revulsion from the actual expressed in the Juvenalian cry, 'How can a man not write satire?' Byron's feelings do not erupt in this way because they are not wholly his own. For this we have the evidence not only of his letters, so full of gaiety and lightness of heart, but also of the poems themselves. For it is a very odd thing that, even at the solemnest moments in these poems, cheerfulness, if it does not quite break in, may at all events be seen not far away.

Consider, for example, the well known passage in Canto III of *Childe Harold* when Byron (no longer disguised as the Childe) declares his sense of unity with the mountains around him:

> I can see
> Nothing to loathe in Nature, save to be
> A link reluctant in the fleshly chain . . .

(III. lxxii)

Here, as in *Lara*, is the irreparable rift in the human personality. But how easily, in this mood, does Byron heal it! Only release the reluctant hold on the flesh, he suggests, and all will be well:

> And when, at length, the mind shall be all free
> From what it hates in this degraded form,
> Reft of its carnal life, save what shall be
> Existent happier in the fly and worm—
> When elements to elements conform,
> And dust is as it should be, shall I not
> Feel all I see, less dazzling, but more warm?
> The bodiless thought? The spirit of each spot,
> Of which, even now, I share at times the immortal lot?

(III. lxxiv)

Byron and the Satiric Temper

No martyr ever looked forward with less apprehension, positively encouraging the worms and decorously settling the dust! This brief Platonic interlude is untypical and hardly convincing, of course, and Byron insisted that the whole Canto was written when he was 'half mad ... between metaphysics, mountains, lakes, love unextinguishable, thoughts unutterable, and the nightmare of my own delinquencies'. He completed the picture by adding, 'I should, many a good day, have blown my brains out, but for the recollection that it would have given pleasure to my mother-in-law' (28 January 1817). Still, the calm, almost cheerful acceptance of an imminent demise seems to have been an important element in his creed. It crops up from time to time in his poetry – as when Conrad refuses Gulnare's help against Seyd and calmly awaits his execution in the morning. Moreover, there is the account in his Letters of the storm at sea off Corfu:

> Fletcher yelled after his wife, the Greeks called on all the saints, the Mussulmans on Alla; the captain burst into tears and ran below deck, telling us to call on God; the sails were split, the main-yard shivered, the wind blowing fresh, the night settling in, and all our chance was to make Corfu, which is in possession of the French, or (as Fletcher pathetically termed it) 'A watery grave'. I did what I could to console Fletcher, but finding him incorrigible, wrapped myself in my Albanian capote ... and lay down on deck to await the worst.
>
> (12 November 1809)

Although such stoical resignation is not itself satirical, one feels that satire is not far off. If life can be surrendered with so little fuss, perhaps it is because it is worthless anyway, because

> When all is won that all desire to woo,
> The paltry prize is hardly worth the cost ...

This mood of the vanity of human wishes was congenial to Byron. As he was to say of Johnson's poem, 'The infinite variety of lives conduct but to death, and the infinity of wishes lead but to disappointment' (Diary, 9 January 1821). It was not a mood of complete pessimism, for the word 'disappointment' implies hope. A little more energy in bringing the shortcoming before the reader would have approached the Juvenalian spirit he aspired to in *English Bards, and Scotch Reviewers*. His claim in that poem that he 'had learned to think and sternly speak the truth' was a youthful delusion. What he did there was to set an ideal in the age of Pope and to blame his contemporaries for falling short of it. But gradually a different attitude supervened in which he saw the ideal as it is, humanly unattainable. The demand for perfection gave way to the acceptance of the truth about life and human nature.

This was the mood of stoical resignation that, in different ways, marked the last phase of the Romantic movement in general. Byron reached it in Canto IV of *Childe Harold*:

> Existence may be borne, and the deep root
> Of life and sufferance makes its firm abode
> In bare and desolated bosoms: mute
> The camel labours with the heaviest load,
> And the wolf dies in silence . . .
>
> (IV. xxi)

It was the end to which the earlier Cantos had been progressing. Now that it was reached, Byron began to feel that he had written himself out. 'I look upon *Childe Harold* as my best,' he wrote to Murray in September 1817, 'and as I begun, I think of concluding with it' (15 September 1817). Yet, although the overall tone of Canto IV is elegiac and stoical, there are noticeable variations, and hints that more does remain to be said. In the midst of his reflections on the ruins of Rome, for example, he speaks of mankind as 'A pendulum betwixt a smile and tear'. But smiles had been generally absent from his longer poems, though plentiful in his letters and the shorter pieces that often accompanied them. When he said he thought of ending with Canto IV he meant that he was done with that vein. 'I am certainly a devil of a mannerist,' he wrote, 'and must leave off . . .' (9 March 1817). In 1814 he had looked at *English Bards* and *The Waltz* and said 'truth to say, my satires are not very playful . . . As to mirth and ridicule, that is out of my way: but I have a tolerable fund of sternness and contempt . . .' (12 March 1814). But the trouble here had been the restrictions of the couplet, and Byron knew it. 'Latterly I can weave a nine-line stanza faster than a couplet, for which I have not the cunning' (26 September 1812), he said. He was well aware of the need for an appropriate verse form. In *Hints from Horace* he warned against a wrong decision and added:

> But lucid order and wit's siren voice
> Await the poet skilful in his choice . . .
> (ll. 63–4)

Nearly all his poetry had been concerned with only one-half of the pendulum's arc; but the 'maddest mirthful mood', so ostentatiously abandoned in *Childe Harold*, was equally important to him. He needed a means of combining the two in his own blend of satire.

In the autumn of 1817, just as he was finishing Canto IV, he discovered J. Hookham Frere's adaption, in his 'Whistlecraft' poem, of the *ottava rima* of Pulci. He seized upon it at once, recognising a subtlety and flexibility capable of capturing every tone of his changing moods. Far from 'leaving off' he was about to realise his greatest achievement.

Beppo, the first poem in the new idiom, is a slight tale, recalling one of the Venetian incidents that had amused Murray. What makes the poem is not the story but the manner of its telling. Still, there is a point worth making about the story itself, for it is the inversion of the Turkish Tales. Beppo, too, has had his share of lurid adventures in the East. But now he has come home, and the adventures, with their accompanying heart-searchings, are of no consequence at all. *They* are not what his wife, Laura, wants to talk about. She is concerned with much more vital matters:

> Beppo! that beard of yours becomes you not,
> It shall be shaved before you're a day older;
> Why do you wear it? O! I had forgot—

> Pray don't you think the weather here is colder?
> How do I look? You shan't stir from this spot
> In that queer dress, for fear that some beholder
> Should find you out, and make the story known.
> How short your hair is! Lord! how grey it's grown!
>
> (xciii)

This is the opposite of Canto IV of *Childe Harold*. It is the acceptance of life not because it is terrible but because it is trivial. The pendulum has completed its swing, and *Beppo* is all on the side of the smile. It has satire, but all extremely good-natured, not seeking 'to think and sternly tell the truth', but to follow the Horatian maxim 'to tell the truth with laughter'. Its objects vary; the main one, perhaps, the difference between life in England and life in Italy. Murray had urged him to exploit this, and he does so without a trace of bitterness, his attitude summed up in a line derived ultimately from Charles Churchill's rather sour poem *The Farewell*,[7] but subsequently softened by Cowper:

> England! with all thy faults I love thee still . . .

The casual tone, the delightful comedy, the digressions and desultory passage from one thing to another, give *Beppo* an ease and urbanity that had always been the mark of Byron's letters, but had hardly yet appeared in his poetry. It was very much a beginning. The new idiom presented Byron at last with the means to be himself, and to express all sides of his variable nature not only in a single poem but almost in a single stanza. And, as he said in the last line of *Beppo*, 'stories somehow lengthen when begun.'

NOTES

1. John Dennis, *The Critical Works*, ed. E. N. Hooker (1939, 1945) II 218–19. Quoted by Ian Jack, *Augustan Satire* (The Clarendon Press, Oxford, 1952) 102–3.
2. William Gifford, *The Baviad and Maeviad*, 8th ed. (John Murray, 1811) 46.
3. Ibid., xi.
4. Lord Byron, *The Poetical Works*, ed. E. H. Coleridge (John

Murray, 1903) I 382.
5 Lord Byron, *Poetical Works*, I 381, *note*.
6 Sir Egerton Brydges, *Letters on the Character and Poetical Genius of Lord Byron* (Longman, Hurst, Rees, Orme, Brown and Green, 1824) 28.
7 Charles Churchill, *The Farewell* (1764) ll. 27–8:

> I hear, and hate—be England what She will,
> With all her faults She is my Country still.

6 THE STYLE OF *DON JUAN* AND AUGUSTAN POETRY[*]

A. B. England

In this essay I want to discuss some of the relationships between Byron's poetic style in *Don Juan* and the English poetry of the early eighteenth century. There has been no extended treatment of the subject since Ronald Bottrall's essay written more than thirty years ago, in which he tried to counteract F. R. Leavis's argument that the relationship between Byron's poetry and that of Pope is not really very close.[1] Although it has become commonplace to mention Byron's intense admiration of Augustan poetry and especially of Pope, nearly all of the comparisons that one encounters are briefly made and undeveloped, usually because the author is concentrating on something else. In making some further comparisons now, I shall be concerned not with matters of direct influence (though evidence of that certainly appears in some of the passages I shall discuss), but with continuities such as those to which T. S. Eliot refers in 'Tradition and the Individual Talent' when he writes that the most 'individual' parts of a poet's work 'may be those in which the dead poets, his ancestors, assert their immortality most vigorously.'[2] To define such continuities is obviously a means of clarifying the place which *Don Juan* occupies in the English literary tradition. And in attempting to do this, I shall introduce a rather different kind of emphasis from that which has so far been prevalent. For it seems to me that the almost exclusive

---

[*] Several parts of this essay also appear in my book, *Byron's Don Juan and Eighteenth-Century Literature* (Bucknell University Press, Lewisburg; Associated University Presses, London, 1974). I am grateful to the editors for permission to reprint. Also, a small part of the essay has appeared in 'World Without Order; Some Thoughts on the Poetry of Swift', *Essays in Criticism,* XVI (1966) 32–43. And I am grateful to the editors of that journal for permission to reprint.

emphasis on Pope has been misplaced, and that the most important connections are with a kind of poetry quite different from his.

I

I do not mean to suggest, however, that the relationship with Pope is inconsiderable. There are moments in *Don Juan*, though they are extremely intermittent, when it is possible to feel a very strong connection between Byron's rhetoric and that of the poet who embodied for him, and still does for us, the central features of the 'Augustan Tradition'. What happens at these moments is that certain types of distinctively Popeian verbal structure are echoed and continued by Byron in a manner that is both less conscious and more subtle than that of his heroic couplet satires, where the imitation of Pope is deliberate and often crude. An example is the following stanza, in which Byron summarises the disorderly career of the average English nobleman:

> They are young, but know not Youth—it is anticipated;
> Handsome but wasted, rich without a sou;
> Their vigour in a thousand arms is dissipated;
> Their cash comes *from*, their wealth goes *to* a Jew;
> Both senates see their nightly votes participated
> Between the Tyrant's and the Tribunes' crew;
> And having voted, dined, drunk, gamed and whored,
> The family vault receives another Lord.
>
> (XI. 75)[3]

From the start of this stanza a high degree of rhetorical order is evident. Byron begins with three carefully balanced antitheses in the first two lines, each stressing that contrast between apparent wealth and real poverty which is at the heart of the stanza's meaning. If we juxtapose with these two lines the following couplet from Pope,

> Fair to no purpose, artful to no end,
> Young without Lovers, old without a Friend,
>
> (*Epistle to a Lady*,
> ll.245–6)[4]

we can see, I think, the kind of pattern from which Byron's derives. In the third line the strictly balanced, divided structure of the first two is loosened, and the words flow freely instead of being organised into epigram. But the free flow that is described is actually enervating and wasteful, and in the next line epigrammatic concision reasserts itself, taking a firm grip on the inanity it delineates. The formal pattern of the rhetoric, with its continuous repetition of structures, has the effect of making the nobleman's decline seem inevitable – the steps in the process of dissolution follow one another as remorselessly as the steps in the progress of the rhetoric. In this stanza, then, an undirected and aimless process of drift is defined by a noticeably purposeful and disciplined verbal pattern. A kind of order is made visible, even tangible, by the shape of the rhetoric. And this rhetorical order both externalises the coherence of the poet's mind and opposes that coherence to the incoherence it defines. In this manner Byron conveys the impression of having achieved an assured moral authority over the chaotic reality he defines.

Very similar effects are achieved in the following passage, where Pope also describes a temporal progression that appears senseless and incoherent:

> Mark by what wretched steps their glory grows,
> From dirt and sea-weed as proud Venice rose;
> In each how guilt and greatness equal ran,
> And all that rais'd the Hero, sunk the Man.
> Now Europe's laurels on their brows behold,
> But stain'd with blood, or ill exchang'd for gold.
>
> (*An Essay on Man*,
> IV, ll. 291–6)

Here again, the disorder which is described is offset by an extraordinary degree of evident order in the poetic style. What Pope

The Style of Don Juan and Augustan poetry

defines is an upward movement towards power and glory which is actually a decline into blood and dirt; an ascent which by any valid standards is really a descent. At every point this incongruity is insisted on, in an elaborate pattern of continuous contrast. In each of the first four lines two apparent opposites are juxtaposed – 'wretched steps'/'glory', 'dirt'/'proud Venice', 'guilt'/'greatness', 'rais'd'/'sunk'. And finally the central contrast between ugliness and magnificence is enforced by the larger unit of the couplet, particularly by the juxtaposition of 'blood' and 'laurels' which that couplet contains.

One can see Byron's rhetoric again working in this manner in his description of Suwarrow:

> Suwarrow chiefly was on the alert,
> Surveying, drilling, ordering, jesting, pondering;
> For the man was, we safely may assert,
> A thing to wonder at beyond most wondering;
> Hero, buffoon, half-demon, and half-dirt,
> Praying, instructing, desolating, plundering—
> Now Mars, now Momus—and when bent to storm
> A fortress, Harlequin in uniform.
>
> (VII. 55)

In the fifth line of this stanza Byron begins to define Suwarrow by means of antithesis. The nouns juxtaposed in the first half of the line are clearly, even diametrically antithetical. But in the second half, while Byron maintains the same rhetorical structure, he does not maintain the apparent clarity of opposition with which he began; for while 'demon' connects with 'Hero' in its connotation of the superhuman, it is obviously not unambiguously admirable. The function of the word's ambiguity, however, is to reflect back critically upon 'Hero' and the concept of heroism, thus complicating but not confusing the satiric force of the antithesis. In the next line the sequence of present participles is organised with a high degree of critical point; the juxtaposition of 'Praying' and 'desolating' clearly defines a deep moral confusion. In the couplet, the contrast between military heroism and comic eccentricity is reinforced by another antithesis, and all the incongruities are finally epitomised in the image of the harlequin. One has only to juxtapose a few lines from Pope's description of Sporus to demonstrate a relationship between Byron's rhetoric here and that of his Augustan predecessor:

> Amphibious Thing! that acting either Part,
> The trifling Head, or the corrupted Heart!
> Fop at the Toilet, Flatt'rer at the Board,
> Now trips a Lady, and now struts a Lord.
> (*Epistle to Dr. Arbuthnot*, ll. 326-9)

And in each instance the act of defining is a way of establishing the author's rhetorical mastery of a chaotic and unruly phenomenon.

The verbal patterns which Pope characteristically constructs tend to imply the existence of an essential order in the nature of things which is obscured by the chaos of what he satirises, and the coherence of the rhetoric is thus related to a vision of order in the universe. What dominates and upholds this vision is a hierarchical value-system that Pope's poetry insistently enforces. The nature of this value-system is well described by Paul Fussell, who says of the English Augustans that 'they inhabit a world where distinction, separation, inequality and hierarchy are self-evident ethical principles.' For them, 'man's obligations to the life of value require of him a constant exercise of hierarchical ranking and arranging of the data of experience.'[5] All of the passages that I have discussed so far enforce one very great hierarchical distinction – that between the coherence embodied by the poem's rhetoric and the disorder of what is being satirised. From these passages certain values such as harmony, balance and congruity emerge as ideal standards by which the satirised objects are judged and towards which the contemplation of these objects leads. It is thus by an emphasis on distinction and separation that the satire in these passages becomes constructive.

Pope's rhetoric constantly implies that particular actions, qualities and characteristics belong to distinct classes or levels in a hierarchical value-system. In the above passage from *An Essay on Man*, the persistent contrasts suggest that in Pope's world certain sharp and clarifying distinctions are available – such as that between genuine greatness and the illusory 'greatness' achieved by the objects of his satire. When Pope says of a man that he desires 'My Friendship, and a Prologue, and ten Pound' (*Epistle to Arbuthnot*, l. 48), he juxtaposes three items which are different in kind so as to define that man's distortion of both personal and literary values. 'Friendship' stands high in Pope's value-system, but in this man's mind it is undistinguished from the giving of favours and the transaction of commerce. He is therefore blind to a distinction which to a rational mind is self-evident. And whereas the mental world of the satirised object is seriously confused, that of the author is coherent because it is informed and sustained by the perception of a hierarchical structure.

One can see a similar kind of world-view asserting itself in Byron's stanza on Suwarrow. There, the definition of Suwarrow's moral confusion is enforced by a line in which he is described as both 'Praying' and 'plundering'. Suwarrow's chaotic nature does not, apparently, recognise any hierarchical or generic difference between the two activities. But the mind of the poet does, and the satirised object is thus evaluated against the background of a value-system that gives order to the poet's world. At another point in *Don Juan* Byron describes Donna Inez setting up a Sunday school so that she may teach children 'to suppress their vice and urine'.[6] The main thrust of this phrase is in its implication of what Donna Inez's mind does to a concept like that denoted by 'vice'. We normally think of vice as being intangible and probably complex, an essentially moral deficiency. But the juxtaposition of words here suggests that Donna Inez regards it as essentially physical, as much a matter of bodily function as 'urine'. And the word cries out against such a reduction and simplification of its meaning. It is clear that the collocation of vice and urine is representative of the way in which Donna Inez, rather than Byron, thinks. So the juxtaposition works to separate the poet from the satirised object, and to imply that his own view of reality is based on his belief in a rational hierarchy. It confirms the reader's assumption that there is a clear distinction between the spiritual and the physical.

II

Although moments like these do occur in *Don Juan*, a major characteristic of the poem's rhetoric is that it tends to undermine the reader's confidence in the kinds of order embodied and suggested by the above structures. While it is important, I think, to recognise the occasions on which the poem's rhetoric is related to Pope's, it also needs to be said that the impulse towards order which those occasions represent appears in a poem which is most of the time imitative of a reality that lacks the coherence in which Pope believed. Therefore, if the style of *Don Juan* is more than sporadically connected with any part of Augustan poetry, that part is not the one represented by Pope. There was, however, a kind of poetry being written in the early eighteenth century which in its style and in the concept of reality implied by that style was radically different from Pope's. And the major practitioner of it was Swift.

Swift's poetry is of course extremely varied, but both he and Pope felt that it tended to possess certain predominant characteristics. And they both referred to these characteristics through the use of the word 'burlesque'. Swift at one point imagines himself being requested to 'suspend a While,/ That same paultry *Burlesque* Stile,'[7] and Pope's list of 'authorities for poetical language' recommended Butler and Swift 'for the burlesque style'.[8] Byron also uses the same word to describe his own poetry in *Don Juan* when he says that 'the sad truth which hovers o'er my desk /Turns what was once romantic to burlesque' (IV.3). Nowadays, of course, the meaning of the word is very generalised, but when Pope and Swift refer to the 'burlesque style' it is clear that they have in mind a fairly definite set of rhetorical expectations. These expectations are based largely on the style of Butler's *Hudibras*, which was widely imitated in the early eighteenth century, and which Swift's poetic manner often resembles. It has been pointed out that burlesque poetry began as an attempt to achieve comic effects by describing the figures and actions of classical epic in a colloquial and vulgar style.[9] And the comedy in *Hudibras* is achieved largely through the juxtaposition of words that possess fairly elevated connotations with words that ordinarily belong to a more commonplace context. The burlesque style thus achieves some of its major effects by exploiting contrasts between radically different kinds of words. But the intention of the burlesque poet, when he juxtaposes kinds and levels, is in no way – as it is in Pope's satires – to criticise failures of discrimination. On the contrary, when the burlesque poet juxtaposes, say, the heroic and the commonplace, his intention is to amuse us by persuading us to entertain the idea of a possible connection between the two. Thus, while the burlesque style is essentially based on the concept of a hierarchical structure, it tends to undermine rather than to affirm that structure.

Swift often uses certain features of the style in his familiar verse, and the following passage illustrates some aspects of his technique:

> But, as for me, who ne'er could clamber high,
> To understand Malebranche or Cambray;
> Who send my mind (as I believe) less
> Than others do, on errands sleeveless;
> Can listen to a tale humdrum,
> And, with attention, read Tom Thumb;
> My spirits with my body progging,
> Both hand in hand together jogging;
> Sunk over head and ears in matter,
> Nor can of metaphysics smatter;
> Am more diverted with a quibble
> Than dreams of worlds intelligible;
> And think all notions too abstracted,
> Are like the ravings of a crackt head;
> What intercourse of minds can be
> Betwixt the Knight sublime and me?
> ('The Dean's Reasons', ll. 51–66)

Here, Swift constantly juxtaposes words that possess strictly physical connotations with words that refer to abstract thought and spiritual experience. And in doing so, he tends to break down rather than to enforce the ordinarily assumed distinctions between those words. The process begins in the first couplet, where the name of a philosopher is rhymed with two words that denote a specifically physical activity. In order to make it rhyme with 'clamber high' the reader unconsciously breaks 'Cambray' into at least two parts, and the word's integrity is thus severely damaged as it is reduced to the status of an object which can be fragmented. Further on, the collocation of 'metaphysics' and 'smatter' is one of a 'high' noun and a 'low' verb, but the context insists that the incongruity between them is only superficial. This distinctively burlesque process is continued in the next couplet, where the commonplace familiarity of 'quibble' brings the soaring implications of 'worlds intelligible' down to its own level. And it is completed by the rhyming of 'abstracted' and 'crackt head', which seems to concentrate within itself all the major tendencies of the passage. For it not only stresses the extreme physicality of that source from which all abstractions must emanate, but it also, by forcing the reader to split 'abstracted' into its component parts, makes him see as a physical object the very word which denotes such abstractions. Throughout the passage Swift's insistence on his own physicality gives the impression that he is sceptical of the well-established hierarchical distinction between mind and body. While the 'Knight sublime' would not question the clarity of this distinction, and would regard it as confirming his sense of his own sublimity, the author seems to perceive a different kind of reality from his – a reality which is so predominantly physical that such distinctions are hard to make.

I would suggest that in the following stanza from *Don Juan* Byron shows an affinity of both style and temperament with the Swift of the above passage:

Her favourite science was the mathematical,
Her noblest virtue was her magnanimity,
Her wit (she sometimes tried at wit) was Attic all,
Her serious sayings darkened to sublimity;
In short, in all things she was fairly what I call
A prodigy—her morning dress was dimity,
Her evening silk, or, in the summer, muslin,
And other stuffs, with which I won't stay puzzling.

(I. 12)

If we look at the sequence, 'mathematical', 'Attic all', 'what I call', we witness a progressive diminution of the power which the first rhyme-word ordinarily has to communicate meaning. For the fragmentation of that word's sound-structure is pushed to such an extreme that the reader is made retrospectively to sense 'mathematical' more strongly as a physical object than as an embodiment of meaning. The rhymes not only damage the word's integrity, they reduce it to the status of a cipher whose meaning is of no account. Such is the kind of thing that tends to happen in this stanza to words denoting those pursuits and talents of which Donna Inez is so proud. It happens in the sequence, 'magnanimity', 'sublimity', 'dimity', where the juxtaposition of the imposingly abstract and the prosaically physical does not imply that any hierarchical distinction needs to be made between them. On the contrary, Byron is throughout the stanza making the point that the 'magnanimity' and the 'sublimity' of Donna Inez are as superficial as the articles of clothing made out of 'dimity', so that the apparently gratuitous details about what she wears in fact follow naturally upon the description of her moral, intellectual and emotional characteristics. Moreover, it is not only Donna Inez's personality which is diminished by this stanza. For when words like 'magnanimity' and 'sublimity' are made to participate in such absurd verbal patterns as this, the dignity and the serious values which are normally attached to them tend to be obscured or even momentarily obliterated. The words appear to be introduced because of their capacity to serve the ends of Byron's verbal farce, and they consequently suffer a reduction — just as in the above passage by Swift, words suggestive of intellectual activity suffer a reduction for the same reason.

The manner in which Swift juxtaposes contrasting items in his poetry constantly tends to undermine hierarchies, and to enforce the concept of an absurd reality in which levels tend to merge rather than to separate. At one point in 'On Poetry: A Rapsody' he suggests that if a satirist does not fully identify the individuals he attacks it will be difficult, merely from a description of their characteristics and activities, to be sure who is referred to:

> A publick, or a private *Robber*;
> A *Statesman*, or a South-Sea *Jobber*.
> A *Prelate* who no God Believes;
> A [Parliament], or Den of Thieves.
> A Pick-purse at the Bar, or Bench;
> A Duchess, or a Suburb-Wench.
>
> (ll. 161–6)

Only a name distinguishes the morally coalescing levels, and if the juxtapositions are incongruous in appearance they are not in fact. Rather than enabling the reader to make clear, confirmatory distinctions, Swift's rhetoric implies that it is hard to separate one level clearly from another, that accepted lines of demarcation are in reality blurred. And the use of juxtaposition here is very much like that which appears time after time in *Don Juan*. A clear example occurs in the first of the following three lines:

> The statesman—hero—harlot—lawyer—ward
> Off each attack, when people are in quest
> Of their designs, by saying they *meant well*.
>
> (VIII. 25)

Byron's point is that all of these apparently disparate kinds of person tend both to do harm and to claim that their good intentions excuse that harm. When he places these items next to one another within the line, therefore, his intention is to suggest that the distinctions between them are not really so clear as they are ordinarily assumed to be. His use of juxtaposition is like Swift's in that it stresses an unrecognised homogeneity beneath the surface differences. A similar effect is given when he writes of the starving Juan:

> He fell upon whate'er was offered, like
> A priest, a shark, an alderman, or pike.
>
> (II. 157)

The second line of this couplet vividly illustrates the difference between the two kinds of juxtaposition that I have been discussing. When Pope places 'Friendship' and 'ten Pound', or bibles and billets-doux close to each other within the poetic line, he is seeking to confirm traditional hierarchic distinctions rather than to imply a real absence of differentiation. The confused surface of his line, in which disparate items are brought unharmoniously together, may imitate the disorder of the satirised object's mind. But there exists for Pope a reality which possesses the order of a hierarchical structure and in which spiritual and materialistic values are clearly separate. His juxtapositions reach beyond the chaotic surfaces he describes to suggest that there is clarity, distinction, coherence in the nature of things. The structure of Byron's line, however, holds 'priest', 'shark', 'alderman' and 'pike' in close conjunction, and he wishes us to see them as being so conjoined in reality; the apparently distinct levels coalesce in fact, not just in the mind of a satirised object who cannot perceive the way things truly are. The juxtapositions do not reach beyond the confused world that they describe towards a coherent ethical structure against the reality of which that world is judged. Rather, the line seems to mimic a reality which is much more deeply disordered than that which Pope perceives, and Byron's juxtapositions offer no reassuring access to a fundamental coherence in the nature of things. They mimic the only reality that the poet knows; they do not ironically define failures to perceive a real hierarchy behind the confusion of immediate particulars.

This distinctively burlesque vision of the world is often expressed by Swift in passages that involve continuous changes of phrase and tone. In his description of 'a Lady's Ivory Table Book', for instance, two apparently disparate kinds of phrase constantly alternate with each other:

> Here you may read (*Dear Charming Saint*)
> Beneath (*A new Receit for Paint*)
> Here in Beau-spelling (*tru tel deth*)
> There in her own (*far an el breth*)
> Here (*lovely Nymph pronounce my doom*)

> There (*A safe way to use Perfume*)
> Here, a Page fill'd with Billet Doux;
> On t'other side (*laid out for Shoes*)
> (*Madam, I dye without your Grace*)
> (*Item, for half a Yard of Lace.*)

The shifting movement of the passage seems to imitate the chaos of the lady's mind. Extreme expressions of romantic love jostle with notes on cosmetics, bad breath, perfume, and the price of shoes. Two voices, that of the beau and that of the lady, sound alternately and create an immediate impression of dissonance through such grating rhymes as 'Billet Doux'/'Shoes' and 'Saint'/'Paint'. But there is a chime of harmony in the second couplet that indicates the way in which the two voices actually blur into each other. For the beau's passion expresses itself in conventionally decorative phrases and goes no deeper than the lady's concern for her recipes. And the final impression is not of contrast between feeling and non-feeling or between the spiritual and the physical, but of uniform sterility. Moreover, no sense is given that the words which the beau uses reach out towards a real world of intense emotional experience that he does not know. All romantic values seem to go down under the weight of their own phrasing and under the pressure of the surrounding context. When Byron describes Don Juan's efforts, in the face of sea-sickness, to assert his continuing devotion to Donna Julia, a similar kind of effect is given:

> 'Sooner shall Heaven kiss earth—(here he fell sicker)
> Oh Julia! what is every other woe?—
> (For God's sake let me have a glass of liquor;
> Pedro, Battista, help me down below.)
> Julia, my love!—(you rascal, Pedro, quicker)—
> Oh, Julia!—(this curst vessel pitches so)—
> Beloved Julia, hear me still beseeching!'
> (Here he grew inarticulate with retching.)
>
> (II.20)

The rhetorical pattern of this stanza is disordered and discontinuous because Byron wants to create the impression that he is directly imitating Juan's chaotic experience. But as in Swift's passage, while two contrasting kinds of diction collide absurdly with each other, the shifting, discontinuous movement of the stanza does not tend to convince us of some more ordered reality in which the kinds of experience juxtaposed here are held clearly distinct. Juan expresses his attachment to Julia, or tries to, in pseudo-poeticisms that do not suggest any very great intensity of feeling. As it is presented in this stanza, therefore, 'love' is not a specially elevated kind of experience, and we are given no sense that, when Juan's expressions of it are juxtaposed with the expressions of his sea-sickness, an extreme discrepancy of hierarchical levels is being stressed. Instead, we are given a sense that reality is so predominantly physical that clear separations are hard to make.

III

In a fairly recent attempt to define the burlesque style, Francis Bar has suggested that one of its major tendencies is to enumerate miscellaneous specifics without organising them into coherent patterns.[10] The device originated as part of the burlesque poet's attempt to create all kinds of discontinuity and incoherence in opposition to the high degree of formal order associated with epic poetry. And a similar kind of stylistic tendency appears in Swift's poetry, often when he is not consciously concerned with being anti-epic. A typical example occurs in 'A Description of a City Shower', where Swift is in fact parodying Virgil's description of a storm in the first book of the *Georgics*, and where the connection with the burlesque tradition is particularly strong:

> To Shops in Crouds the daggled Females fly,
> Pretend to cheapen Goods, but nothing buy.
> The Templer spruce, while ev'ry Spout's a-broach,
> Stays till 'tis fair, yet seems to call a Coach.
> The tuck'd-up Sempstress walks with hasty Strides,
> While Streams run down her oil'd Umbrella's Sides.
> Here various Kinds by various Fortunes led,

>   Commence Acquaintance underneath a Shed.
>   Triumphant Tories, and desponding Whigs,
>   Forget their Fewds, and join to save their Wigs.
>
>   (ll. 33-42)

Here, Swift enumerates the various items in such a way as to avoid any ethical or thematic classification of them. There is, of course, a kind of relationship between the various individuals in that they all have a common purpose. But this is a superficial, fortuitous connection, and the passage is carefully organised to give the impression that the speaker is observing quite randomly, noting items without selecting or ordering them. Because of this it seems inappropriate to define the succession of items in the way it is defined by the following statement; 'the city's corruption is betokened . . . in the behaviour of the citizens caught in the downpour. Hypocrisy, or falseseeming, is the essence of their natures. Tories and Whigs, in the face of the threatening deluge, discard their ostensibly principled differences and reveal their true common purposes.'[11] Such ethical classification of the poem's various details has the effect of attributing to them a much greater degree of generic life than they actually have. It simply cannot be assumed that a series of particulars in Swift's poetry is likely to possess the kind of morally significant coherence that such series do in Pope's. In this instance Swift is intent on preserving the sheer miscellaneousness of the juxtaposed items, and they are not allowed to participate in any significant patterns of generic contrast or similarity. His picture shows no evidence of coherent composition, and its specific elements seem likely to spill over the edges of any frame that might irrelevantly be imposed on them.

In the second canto of *Don Juan*, when he describes the multitudinous chaos wrought by the storm at sea, Byron also accumulates particulars without forming them into coherently thematic patterns:

>   Some went to prayers again, and made a vow
>   Of candles to their saints—but there were none
>   To pay them with; and some look'd o'er the bow;

The Style of Don Juan and Augustan poetry

> Some hoisted out the boats;and there was one
> That begged Pedrillo for an absolution,
> Who told him to be damned—in his confusion.
>
> Some lashed them in their hammocks; some put on
> Their best clothes, as if going to a fair;
> Some cursed the day on which they saw the Sun,
> And gnashed their teeth, and howling, tore their hair.
>
> (II. 44–5)

The items in this passage are carefully selected so as to give the impression that no process of selection has gone on, and they are arranged in a sequence which gives the impression that they have not been arranged at all. Only in the first two lines of the second stanza, with their juxtaposition of the private and the public, do we find items achieving a degree of relationship with each other through the principle of generic contrast. Elsewhere, they appear to stand next to one another only because they do so in that actuality which Byron's rhetorical pattern imitates, and which he purports to register by a process of random notation. Especially in the movement from those who 'went to prayers' to those who 'looked o'er the bow' there is a studied discontinuity, a lack of significant progression. And the reference to the second of these two groups of people is ostentatiously gratuitous; by simply looking 'o'er the bow' they take on no generic or otherwise significant life, and Byron creates the illusion that he points them out only because they are there. Byron's rhetorical structure, therefore, is designed so as to appear to be inclusive of individual items which not only enforce no theme, but do not even belong to any ordered world of kinds. And the movement between these disconnected particulars is as imitatively discontinuous as that in 'A Description of a City Shower'.

In passages like this, it is made to appear that an unstructured external reality finds its way, unorganised and untransformed, into the fabric of Byron's poetry. No evident design within the rhetoric opposes itself to or resists the chaotic multiplicity that is being presented. And this stylistic tendency becomes especially noticeable when the subject matter which is being treated is of a dull or repetitive nature. We see a vivid instance when Byron describes the life of the old people at Norman Abbey:

> The elderly walked through the library,
> And tumbled books, or criticised the pictures,
> Or sauntered through the garden piteously,
> And made upon the hot-house several strictures,
> Or rode a nag which trotted not too high,
> Or on the morning papers read their lectures,
> Or on the watch their longing eyes would fix,
> Longing at sixty for the hour of six.
>
> (XIII. 102)

And we see another instance when Swift describes the daily routine of the visitors to Market Hill, especially of 'Heteroclit Dan',

> Who neither time nor order kept.
> But by peculiar Whimseys drawn,
> Peeps in the Ponds to look for Spawn;
> O'er sees the Work, or *Dragon* rowes,
> Or spoils a Text or mends his Hose.
> Or—but proceed we in our *Journal*
> At Two or after we return all.
>
> ('The Journal', ll. 20–26)

In each case the movement of the lines seems intended to reproduce in a fairly direct way the monotony and the repetitiveness of what is being described. In response to a life-style which is a shapeless succession of dull alternatives the poet constructs a rhetorical pattern which is itself characterised by a similar kind of inconsequence. And in doing this he creates the impression that he is enumerating events rather than transforming them under the pressure of a defining thematic vision.

Don Juan is, of course, an extremely varied poem, and it is not dominated by any one style. But the kind of rhetoric I have described in comparing Byron with Swift appears much more frequently than that which I described in comparing Byron with

Pope, and it is more central to the poem in that it is closely related to the kind of world-view which *Don Juan* as a whole tends to enforce. I have tried to describe some aspects of what I take to be a genuine stylistic continuity, and one which connects both Swift and Byron with the tradition of English burlesque poetry. In order to demonstrate a continuity rather than an influence, one does not, I suppose, need to have evidence that Byron was particularly familiar with Swift's poetry. But on separate occasions in his letters Byron quotes casually from 'Clever Tom Clinch' and 'The Grand Question Debated', two of Swift's lesser-known poems.[12] And what these occasions indicate, I think, is that although Byron did not talk about Swift's poetry as much as he did about Pope's, he did in fact know it rather well.

NOTES

1. Ronald Bottrall, 'Byron and the Colloquial Tradition in English Poetry', *Criterion* XVIII (1939) 204–24. F. R. Leavis, *Revaluation* (Chatto and Windus: London, 1936) 148–53.
2. *Selected Essays*, 3rd ed. (Faber and Faber, London, 1958) 14.
3. Quotations are from *The Works of Lord Byron, Poetry*, ed. E. H. Coleridge, 7 vols (London, 1898–1904).
4. Quotations are from the one-volume Twickenham edition, *The Poems of Alexander Pope*, ed. John Butt (New Haven, Conn. 1963).
5. *The Rhetorical World of Augustan Humanism* (Oxford, 1965) 119.
6. Cancelled couplet of II, 10. Given in *Byron's Don Juan: A Variorum Edition*, ed. Truman Guy Steffan and Willis W. Pratt, 4 vols (Austin, Texas, 1957) II 162.
7. 'An Epistle to a Lady', l. 50. Quotations are from *The Poems of Jonathan Swift*, ed. Harold Williams, 2nd ed., 3 vols (Oxford, 1958).
8. Joseph Spence, *Observations, Anecdotes, and Characters of Books and Men*, ed. James M. Osborn, 2 vols (Oxford, 1966) I 171.
9. Ruth Nevo, *The Dial of Virtue: A Study of Poems on Affairs of State In the Seventeenth Century* (Princeton, 1963) 189.
10. *Le Genre Burlesque en France au XVII siècle* (Paris, 1960) 351.

11 Brendan O Hehir, 'Meaning in Swift's "Description of a City Shower"', *ELH*, XXVII (1960) 194–207.
12 *Byron: A Self-Portrait*, ed. Peter Quennell, 2 vols (John Murray, London, 1950) II 404, 705.

7 DON JUAN IN SEARCH OF FREEDOM: BYRON'S EMERGENCE AS A SATIRIST

W. Ruddick

The best possible introduction and ideal companion to the poetry of Lord Byron is a good annotated selection from his letters. Throughout his life Byron was a highly autobiographical, almost impulsively confessional writer in both his prose and his poetry, and comparisons between the two will continually reveal the basic consistency and high quality of his imagination and thinking. But such comparisons will also reveal differences of approach and presentation, not due to basic changes in Byron's thinking but imposed on his verse (for it is a one-way process by which his epistolary prose is unaffected) by preconceived notions of literary decorum from which he only escaped towards the end of his writing career.

Almost all of Byron's letters reveal a completely integrated, highly spontaneous gift for self-expression. Even letters written in his early manhood demonstrate the characteristic rapidity of movement from absurdity to seriousness, sentiment to satire, and the ability of the assured authorial voice to encompass every tone from the tender to the devastatingly dismissive which we associate with his best mature satiric poetry. But in the field of poetry the state of affairs is very much less satisfactory. Byron's poems show clear signs of divided aims and unresolved tensions within his personality throughout much of his writing career. It is only in his final satires (*Beppo, Don Juan, The Vision of Judgment*) that he achieves an adequate synthesis of all his gifts in poetry: and even here most critics hold some reservations concerning the security or completeness of his success.

The reasons for Byron's inability to express his complete

viewpoint and emotional range within the confines of a single poem until a late stage of his career seem worth pursuing. He could be violently changeable in mood and was often driven to voice extreme or conflicting opinions through the urgency of his need to find self-expression, yet at bottom he was sufficiently stable to be in command of his own, highly characteristic voice as a prose writer while still an undergraduate. That he should have had to wait till almost thirty years of age before mastering the art of complete self-portraiture in verse suggests that something was seriously amiss. In attempting to locate the source of his difficulties (which were far more of an artistic than a psychological nature) his attitudes to the writing of satire and achievements in that genre are of particular importance. His early satirical writing highlights the nature of his problems, and it was in satirical writing that he eventually triumphed over them.

Many of the poems which Byron wrote before discovering how to embody the whole of his complex nature in poetry are works of considerable stature. *Childe Harold, Manfred* and *The Prisoner of Chillon* all possess strong claims to our attention. But when read beside Byron's letters or journals of the same date the poems almost invariably suggest a powerful imagination being hampered in its work by emotional and stylistic restrictions. The form which Byron has chosen limits the amount of perception which can be introduced within it. In addition, where two or more contemporary poems in contrasting idioms exist, they almost invariably look less like poems capable of standing alone than parts of a single imaginative response when seen alongside the more integrated record preserved by prose writings from the same period. The letters or journal entries appear to be free from literary convention: they also possess a power to move among contrasting areas of experience without discernible strain, which emphasises the degree to which conventional limitations of approach or restrictions on the subject matter exert an impoverishing effect on Byron's poetry.

To instance this impoverishment, a letter which Byron wrote in August 1810 during his residence in Athens may be set against some of the poetry which he wrote during the same period. At this date Byron was living in a somewhat disreputable monastery, richly enjoying the absurd contrasts provided by the city's social, political and amorous activities. He writes to his friend and former travelling companion John Cam Hobhouse, and in the satiric relationship and tone of voice which he adopts, Hobhouse is visualised as the prototype Byronic auditor: shockable, slightly parochial, yet unable to break away from the siren voice which regales him with such enchantingly ridiculous, often salacious titbits of news:

> I have girated the Morea, and was presented with a very fine horse (a stallion) and honoured with a number of squeezes and speeches by Velly Pacha, besides a most pressing invitation to meet him at Larissa in his way to the wars . . .
>
> But my friend as you may easily imagine is Nicolo, who by the bye, is my Italian master, and we are already very philosophical. – I am his 'Padrone' and his 'amico' and the Lord knows what besides, it is about two hours since that after informing me he was most desirous to follow *him* (that is me) over the world, he concluded by telling me it was proper for us not only to live but 'morire insieme'. – The latter I hope to avoid, as much of the former as he pleases . . .
>
> Then we have several Albanian women washing in the 'giardino' whose hours of relaxation are spent in running pins into Fletcher's backside . . .
>
> I am learning Italian, and this day translated an ode of Horace 'Exegi monumentum' into that language . . .
>
> Lord Sligo . . . is now at Argos with his hospital but intends to winter in Athens. I think he will be sick of it, poor soul he has all the indecision of your humble servant, without the relish for the ridiculous which makes my life supportable.
>
> (23 and 24 August 1810)

In the various poems which Byron wrote during his stay in Athens his 'relish for the ridiculous' tends to be kept well in check by the self-dramatisation and political earnestness of *Childe Harold* (the humorous, satiric element in the first two Cantos was never strong and was further weakened by excisions) or put in a straight-jacket by Popean satiric conventions as in *Hints from Horace* (while the unfortunate *Curse of Minerva* was strangled by both). The freedom of a letter, in which Byron can be translating Horace at one moment and vowing love eternal with important mental reservations the next, disappears: analogous experiences are rigidly segregated according to whether they seem best suited to a dramatic or satirical method of presentation.

In *Childe Harold* and *Hints from Horace* Byron does indeed deal with many directly comparable experiences. As representative examples we may consider two short passages, one from each poem. In the first Byron stands on the Acropolis and dreams of its vanished glories: his reverie is disturbed by the recollection that some of the glories vanished very recently indeed, *en route* for London in the holds of Lord Elgin's ships:

> Here let me sit upon this massy stone,
> The marble column's yet unshaken base;
> Here, son of Saturn! was thy favourite throne:
> Mightiest of many such! Hence let me trace
> The latent grandeur of thy dwelling-place.
> It may not be: nor ev'n can Fancy's eye
> Restore what Time hath laboured to deface.
> Yet these proud Pillars claim no passing sigh;
> Unmoved the Moslem sits, the light Greek carols by.
>
> But who, of all the plunderers of yon Fane
> On high – where Pallas linger'd, loth to flee
> The latest relic of her ancient reign –
> The last, the worst, dull spoiler, who was he?
> Blush, Caledonia! such thy son could be! . . .
>
> (*Childe Harold's Pilgrimage*, II.x–xi)

In the second passage Byron again stands on a historic site and has his romantic musings shattered by the memory of Scottish iniquity: the sin, this time, being that of Francis Jeffrey, editor of the *Edinburgh Review*, whom Byron believed to be responsible for a scathing review of *Hours of Idleness*, his first published volume of poetry:

> Is it for this on Ilion I have stood,
> And thought of Homer less than Holyrood?
> On shore of Euxine or Aegean sea,
> My hate, untravelled, fondly turned to thee.
> Ah! let me cease! in vain my bosom burns,
> From Corydon unkind Alexis turns.
> (*Hints from Horace*, ll.615–20)

These two passages come from very different poems. *Childe Harold* is a 'Romaunt' or lay, in which the story exists only to provide the sketchy framework for a travel journal of evocations and personal impressions. *Hints from Horace* is a literary and social satire in the manner of Gifford and Pope in which Byron buries some interesting passages of personal revelation beneath a mass of second-hand ruminations in the old Augustan manner of moral generalisation. In neither poem can Byron write freely about himself (though the rhapsodic form of *Childe Harold*, little restricted by literary precedent, allows him to do so for long stretches before the story reclaims his attention) for the classification of material into serious and satiric imposed by his acceptance of rigid literary conventions also restricts the degree to which he can abandon himself to self-revelation. Yet the two passages quoted above are indicative of the degree to which his own responses lie at the heart of the poetry written while he was in Greece. The Athenian and the Trojan experiences are complementary in the two kinds of response to historic stimuli which they show. The one is patriotic, the other comic, and hence the dictates of eighteenth-century poetry keep them apart, destroying in the process the possibilities for ironic interplay which we have already seen in Byron's Athenian letter. By accepting conventional ideas about poetic genres at this period Byron impoverishes his poetry. It was only when he learned to rethink the meaning of Pope and Augustan satire that he was able, in his late satires, to display the full richness of life, personal reactions and the satiric experience.

Byron had begun writing poetry in the opening years of the nineteenth century, at a time when the full impact of Romantic poetry had hardly begun to affect English readers or the vast majority of English writers. His earliest poems are facile exercises in the elegant, lightweight, sentimental and amorous modes popularised by Thomas Moore's first volumes. The understandably mocking review of his *Hours of Idleness* in the *Edinburgh Review* for January 1808 stimulated a latent gift for satire; Byron found that, like his idol Pope, he was not only a good but also an effective hater. *English Bards, and Scotch Reviewers* shows that though Byron may be imitating Pope for much of the time, he is at least imitating him with spirit: as when he ridicules the idea of yet another epic from the over-productive muse of Robert Southey:

> Oh, Southey! Southey! cease thy varied song!
> A bard may chaunt too often and too long:
> As thou art strong in verse, in mercy, spare!
> A fourth, alas! were more than we could bear.
> (*English Bards, and Scotch Reviewers*, ll.225–8)

The decorous, eighteenth-century insultingness of the language ('cease thy *varied* song' or the transformation worked on 'strong in arms' in the third line) links Byron to a good old tradition. But a modern reader is likely to be more struck by the quality of farcical mockery (a combination of superciliousness and sheer cheek) which appears in the best passages of the poem. Turning Wordsworth into the hero of *The Idiot Boy* for instance:

> Next comes the dull disciple of thy school,
> That mild apostate from poetic rule,
> The simple Wordsworth, framer of a lay
> As soft as evening in his favourite May,
> Who warns his friend 'to shake off toil and trouble,

And quit his books, for fear of growing double;'
Who, both by precept and example, shows
That prose is verse, and verse is merely prose;
Convincing all, by demonstration plain,
Poetic souls delight in prose insane;
And Christmas stories tortured into rhyme
Contain the essence of the true sublime.
Thus, when he tells the tale of Betty Foy,
The idiot mother of 'an idiot Boy;'
A moon-struck, silly lad, who lost his way,
And, like his bard, confounded night with day;
So close on each pathetic part he dwells,
And each adventure so sublimely tells,
That all who view the 'idiot in his glory'
Conceive the Bard the hero of the story.
  (*English Bards, and Scotch Reviewers*, ll. 235–54)

The 'succès de scandale' achieved by *English Bards, and Scotch Reviewers* was enough to encourage Byron's satiric muse to further flights in the Popean manner. *Hints from Horace*, the poem which he thought of as the most serious fruit of his residence in Greece (till the remarks of his friends led him to publish *Childe Harold* first instead), is intended to act as a continuation of *English Bards, and Scotch Reviewers* and to embody a wider survey of English literature and society. But even a cursory glance at it will reveal why Byron found it necessary to write *Childe Harold* at the same time. In both poems the basic impulse is autobiographical: the young writer on the threshold of his career, enabled by absence from England and exposure to foreign culture to take a fresh look at his original environment, feels the need to analyse society and his own relationship to it. The same situation arose again after Byron left England on the breakdown of his marriage, and again he was at first unable to achieve an integrated poetical form for personal expression. In 1817–18 he at last did so with *Beppo* and *Don Juan*. In 1811 any integrated form of self-exploration other than in prose eluded him. The path from *Hints from Horace* to *Don Juan* involved a radical rethinking of the nature of tradition in satiric writing, and it is this process which must now be examined.

Hints from Horace and *The Waltz* (written in 1812, before the success of *Childe Harold* had reconciled him to the excesses of London society) are frustrating works. A great deal of sensitive, needle-sharp perception of how the world runs, and how badly, can be found in them; as in Byron's description of London's growth:

> Our giant Capital, whose squares are spread
> Where rustics earned, and now may beg, their bread,
> In all iniquity is grown so nice,
> It scorns amusements which are not of price.
> 			(*Hints from Horace*, ll. 303–6)

But the personal voice is constantly lost amid dull echoes of Pope and Gifford:

> I loathe an Opera worse than Dennis did;
> Where good and evil persons, right or wrong,
> Rage, love and aught but moralise – in Song.
> 			(*Hints from Horace*, ll. 296–8)

Throughout his career Byron felt impelled to preserve Augustan standards of taste which he had partly absorbed through his education and his reading of the classics, but more directly derived (and kept nourished) from his love of the poetry of Pope. The standards of Popean satire were large and flexible enough to embrace the new experiences and sensibilities of Regency England (as Jane Austen was demonstrating even while Byron was writing), but the technical features of Popean satire were obsolescent. The effects of this are obvious in Byron's writing at this period. His familiar prose, where archaic concepts of form do not trouble him, succeeds perfectly in preserving its satirical stance along with Romantic sensitivity. The stylistic features of the old satiric verse school are inadequate. Constant antithetical division of issues within the couplet, assertive statement, the condensation of analysis and crystallisation of its results into generalisation; above all the remorseless demand for fixity and precision; these place an intolerable burden upon the writer trying to capture the Romantic sense of complexity, flow and flux in human experience.

The youthful Byron who lambasted Wordsworth and Coleridge in *English Bards, and Scotch Reviewers,* holding up Pope and Goldsmith (the only two perfect English poets, he was to write on 23 April 1820) as the guardians of true tradition in poetry, was himself far too sensitive and complex a man to remain untouched by the aesthetic advances of his age. Indeed his praise of Goldsmith is symptomatic: he responds to both technique and emotional colouring in Goldsmith's poetry. Goldsmith was one of the founding fathers of the school of sentimentalist writers which grew up in the later eighteenth century. Byron was deeply attuned to their work, and in particular to Sterne's fusion of sentiment and ironic psychological presentation in the narrator figures of *Tristram Shandy* and *A Sentimental Journey,* without which the narrator of *Don Juan* could scarcely have come into existence. But more fundamentally still he responded to the Romantic stress on the individual sensibility's right to concentrate egocentrically on the significance of personal experience and its attendant insights. Also, he was deeply imbued with the new sense of history and the continuity of time, relating present experience to that of the past and linking present culture to that of former ages, which Scott was embodying in his verse tales and would shortly develop still further in fiction.

As Byron's need to augment his satirical writing with the confessional *Childe Harold* shows, the old school of satirical writing could no longer cope with these new ways of seeing experience. Eighteenth-century satire was static, Romantic feeling dynamic. A form which could give satire a sense of flow and forward movement was urgently needed. It took Byron a long time to understand this, for like all satiric poets of that period he did not realise that the process of adapting older ways of presentation to the demands of a changed society, which Dryden and Pope had effected by bringing the methods of Horace and Juvenal up to date for Augustan society, was once again essential. The situation has its own deep ironies, for it was largely Byron's misplaced respect for the techniques (as distinct from the standards) of Pope and his followers that prevented him from doing what was necessary much earlier. He already had in his hands the darts most likely to do damage in the Regency or Romantic context: he merely needed to be convinced it was lawful to fling them.

Even before the period when Byron's division of himself between *Childe Harold* and the Popean satires reveals the growing cleft between what he had to say and the literary modes traditionally available for self-expression, he had demonstrated how satire, delicacy of insight and sheer speed of impact could go together in poetry. As he and his companions set off from Falmouth in June 1809 the absurdities of the scene inspired him to dash off a comic account in a verse letter to his friend the Reverend Francis Hodgson. The *Lines to Mr. Hodgson. Written on Board the Lisbon Packet* are reminiscent of Smollett and Rowlandson in their farcicality and vigour, but their rapid presentation of the confused and (mostly) terrified mental states of the whole party offers the earliest indication in Byron's poetry (as distinct from his letters, where such gifts were never absent) of the quick timing and comic undercutting which he made essential features of the satire in *Don Juan*:

> ... Now we've reached her, lo! the Captain,
> *Gallant* Kidd, commands the crew
> Passengers *now* their berths are clapt in,
> Some to grumble, some to spew,
> Heyday! call you that a Cabin?
> Why tis hardly three feet square
> Not enough to stow Queen Mab in,
> Who the deuce can harbour there?
> Who Sir? plenty
> Nobles twenty
> Did at once my vessel fill
> Did they — Jesus!
> How you squeeze us
> Would to God, they did so still,
> Then I'd scape the heat & racket
> Of the good ship, Lisbon Packet.

> Fletcher, Murray, Bob, where are you?
> Stretched along the deck like logs
> Bear a hand – you jolly tar you!
> Here's a rope's end for the dogs,
> Hobhouse muttering fearful curses
> As the hatchway down he rolls
> Now his breakfast, now his verses
> Vomits forth & damns our souls,
> Here's a stanza
> On Braganza
> Help! – a couplet – no, a cup
> Of warm water,
> What's the matter?
> Zounds! my liver's coming up,
> I shall not survive the racket
> Of this brutal Lisbon Packet.
>
> (30 June 1809)

The success of *Childe Harold* and his friends' poor opinion of the satires he had brought back from abroad led Byron to concentrate on Romantic tales and lyrics for some years after 1812. But during this period, while he was being lionised by London society and storing up experience which was to lie at the heart of *Don Juan*, his attitude to Pope and Popean satire underwent an important change.

This change owed a great deal to Thomas Moore. In 1811 Byron formed a personal friendship with the Irish poet whose love verses had exerted a strong influence on his own youthful work. Moore's career offers interesting parallels with Byron's: a few years Byron's senior, he had already gone through his own phase of Popean satiric imitation and was now developing a light, urbane, rapid-paced and aristocratically toned satire of a kind which was genuinely new.

In 1813 Moore's *Twopenny Post-Bag*, a series of verse letters pouring scorn on the Regent and his ministers, scored an immediate success. Byron read it with immense enjoyment, and the fact that he instantly began quoting from it and imitating particular parts of it in letters to his friends shows how deeply it impressed him.

The best of all Byron's imitations of Moore comes in a letter to his publisher, John Murray, and was written a little after this period. It may, however, be quoted because it shows how thoroughly Byron mastered the characteristics of Moore's satirical style and then surpassed the already considerable achievement of his master.

Moore's letter from a bookseller to a hapless author, politely declining to publish his manuscript (the seventh letter in *The Twopenny Post-Bag*) and Byron's *Epistle from Mr. Murray to Dr. Polidori* are rather too long to be quoted in full here. This is unfortunate, since both are very entertaining, each has distinctive merits of its own, and close comparison reveals how much Byron found in Moore that was congenial and could serve as a jumping-off ground for his own imagination. The closeness of the two writers can be seen in a comparison of the respective passages in which the booksellers urge their aspiring authors to try their hands at something else:

> An East-India pamphlet's a thing that would tell—
> And a lick at the Papists is sure to sell well.
> Or—supposing you've nothing *original* in you—
> Write Parodies, Sir, and such fame it will win you,
> You'll get to the Blue-stocking Routs of Albinia!
>
> (Moore)

> The *Quarterly*—Ah, Sir, if you
> Had but the Genius to review!—
> A smart Critique upon St. Helena,
> Or if you only would but tell in a
> Short compass what—but to resume;
> As I was saying, Sir. . . .
>
> (Byron)

But all the way through one is conscious of how Byron deepens the sense of drama and personal relationships within the situation:

> Per post, Sir, we send your MS.—look'd it thro'—
> Very sorry—but can't undertake—'twouldn't do.
> Clever work, Sir!—would *get up* prodigiously well—
> Its only defect is—it never would sell.
> (Moore)

> Dear Doctor, I have read your play,
> Which is a good one in its way,—
> Purges the eyes, and moves the bowels,
> And drenches handkerchiefs like towels
> With tears, that, in a flux of grief,
> Afford hysterical relief
> To shattered nerves and quickened pulses,
> Which your catastrophe convulses . . .
> It is not that I am not sensible
> To merits in themselves ostensible,
> But—and I grieve to speak it—plays
> Are drugs—mere drugs, Sir—now-a-days.
> (Byron)

Byron's debts to Moore have received less consideration than they deserve. It is true, of course, that reading the *Twopenny Post-Bag* and its successors mattered less to Byron than his reading of Pulci and John Hookham Frere's *Whistlecraft* when he came to write *Beppo* and *Don Juan*. The Italian medley poets and their English imitator taught him how a long, discursive poem about contemporary life could be tackled and gave him the ideal stanza to do it with. But Moore's lesson was also a valuable one. He showed Byron how the kind of impromptu-seeming, rapid, diverse poems he had till then thought of as mere vehicles for the entertainment of close friends could be fit media for satirical public statements. Byron learned from Moore that the standards of Pope could be embodied in verse whose tone and range of reference accorded closely with the fashionable culture of Regency England. He showed Byron, too, how to use the style and standards of Regency gentlemen as vehicles for satirical comment. It was from Moore, indeed, that Byron learned how to give the man of the world who constantly features in his letters a local habitation and a tone of voice within his satires. And finally, even before he tried the *ottava rima* stanza, Byron had discovered from Moore's work that a lighter, more rapid rhythm such as Moore's favourite anapaest was a better medium for contemporary satire than the well-tried (and by now well-worn) iambic pentameters of the heroic couplet.

At first Byron only used the devices he was learning from Moore in short pieces of verse enclosed in letters to his friends, as he had earlier done with the verse letter to Francis Hodgson. But the change over from private to public light verse came about when Byron, who had been forced into exile by the scandal following the breakdown of his marriage in 1816, began to use his letters to Murray as semi-public documents, intended to be passed round among his friends. Indeed direct proof of this exists in the fact that Byron's letter to Murray dated 8 February 1822, which he authorised Murray to circulate, was versified in the *Don Juan* style by 'Ensign Odoherty' (J. G. Lockhart?) in *Blackwood's Magazine* (March 1822). The various verse letters to Murray were intended for more than the publisher's eye alone, and their satiric thrusts intended to amuse a larger audience. By 1817 when Byron was at last relatively settled once again in Venice he was in a position analogous to that in which he had found himself during his Athenian residence of 1811: alone, outside English society and urgently needing to rethink his relations with it, presented with a discordant mass of experience which defied harmonisation (how, after all, to harmonise the hypocrisy and inhumanity, as it seemed to him, of his treatment before leaving England?) and could only be analysed through satire and its assumptions. But, whereas in 1811 his poetical personality had divided under the strain, he was now ready, thanks to the example of Moore, to write a satirical poem truly contemporary in its methods and terms of reference. The skills which he had been keeping in good order in his prose and short comic poems during the years following the publication of *Childe Harold*, when his published work, though voluminous, contained nothing that could be called directly satirical, were now free to operate without the shackles of outmoded poetic codes of procedure. And finally the Italian medley poets offered him a form analogous to that of English eighteenth-century satirical fiction in which the diversity and complex reality of experience could be given the necessary qualities of freedom and forward movement.

Beppo, the Venetian story celebrating Italian amatory conventions (and obliquely but unceasingly ridiculing the more rigid ones which had victimised Byron and necessitated his Italian exile), and the early cantos of *Don Juan*, the vast poem which Byron began to write when *Beppo* proved successful, have been sufficiently discussed and written about to require little treatment here. In these poems Byron breaks clean away from Popean models at last. The manner is now narrative instead of statically analytical. Instead of being perpetually checked and held in balance, the verse flows forward towards the clinching or debunking couplet at the end of each eight-lined stanza. The authorial voice is no longer that of an insecure Juvenal, undernourished by contact with living thought and imagination, but that of the alert, amused, clear-sighted and only superficially blasé narrator who is already familiar from Byron's letters and impromptu verses. Above all, the Byronic narrator is now a man conscious of his relationship to the moral and psychological traditions of a living, European (if not, indeed, extra-European in the Turkish parts of *Don Juan*), Liberal and still developing culture. Against this stands the narrow parochialism of English society and it is into the dark places of Regency society and the Regency psyche that Byron casts his warm, clear European light.

One other point should be made about these first works of Byron's full maturity. In losing his excessive respect for older models Byron also gained the freedom to treat them as materials for ironic comedy. In itself, of course, this marks a return to the freedom to reshape earlier literary models for contemporary satiric purposes which Dryden and Pope had possessed but which had been lost beneath the excessive respectfulness of later eighteenth-century writers. In *The Rape of the Lock* and *The Dunciad* Pope remoulded epic models and enriched traditional genres in his satire (as when he added Spenserian to Ovidian associations in the

Cave of Spleen episode). Even before this we find the same process taking place in Milton, who fuses earlier, divergent traditions in his accounts of Hell or Paradise so as to give universal applicability and relevance to his myth.

Byron's *Don Juan* marks a recovery of this tradition in satire after a period of timid respectfulness. The myth of Don Juan, in its transformed Byronic form, is altered so that the active libertine of Molière's and Mozart's dramas (the first a political libertine or free-thinker, the second sexually so) becomes a largely passive sufferer of the stresses and distortions imposed upon a sensitive character by early nineteenth-century society and its mores in various parts of Europe. In itself this change to a passive, receptive hero demonstrates Byron's sensitivity to contemporary shifts of feeling and the need for new literary procedures to deal with them. Such analogous manifestations as the politically passive, widely-sympathising heroes of Scott's novels or the choice of largely passive heroines in Jane Austen's two most advancedly Romantic novels *Persuasion* and *Mansfield Park* spring to mind at this point. The means Byron uses to universalise his myth extend not only to the story, with its shifting scenes both within and outside Europe, but also to the form of his narrative and the literary genres which it draws together within its episodes. In these late poems the eighteenth-century divisions between kinds of narrative such as the epic, lyrical and satirical merge and are fused. The early cantos of *Don Juan*, for instance, can reconcile an overall framework of epic parody (including such reworkings of epic situations as the storm at sea or the siege of Ismail) with the delicate lyricism of Juan and Haidée's love affair on the island or the operatic imbroglios of his very first love-affair with Donna Julia. In this his initial resemblance to Mozart's Cherubino itself suffers a sea change to be finally submerged in an ensemble of farcical Rossinian clatter:

> Dire was the scuffle, and out went the light;
> Antonia cried out 'Rape!' and Julia 'Fire!'
> But not a servant stirred to aid the fight.
> Alfonso, pommelled to his heart's desire,
> Swore lustily he'd be revenged this night;

> And Juan, too, blasphemed an octave higher;
> His blood was up: though young, he was a Tartar,
> And not at all disposed to prove a martyr.
>
> (*Don Juan*, I. clxxxiv)

In less than a dozen stanzas the tone can subside from this lively farce to the delicate sentimentality of Julia's farewell letter ('Man's love is of man's life a thing apart,/'Tis Woman's whole existence'), modulating via Juan's mother who, to 'divert' the scandal, offers the Virgin Mary 'several pounds of candles'. And whether satirical or sentimental, the tone of an incident or its apparent significance in the epic or absurd situation is liable to be transformed at any moment by the interjections of Byron's worldly-wise narrator. Or an effect may be scuttled from below by the absurd bathetic power of one of Byron's final couplets:

> 'Belovéd Julia, hear me still beseeching!'
> (Here he grew inarticulate with retching.)
>
> (*Don Juan*, II. xx)

The way in which Byron uses his pictures of European life and manners in the first half of *Don Juan* to cast ironic light on a whole complex of English evasions and hypocrisies (which he sums up by the single word 'cant') has been well discussed by his critics. But faced by the second half of the poem, in which Juan arrives in England to experience fashionable aristocratic life in London and the big country houses, most writers on Byron become more hesitant. Partly this is due to the obvious difficulty that Byron starts a story of romantic intrigue moving, involving Juan's hostess, the seemingly-glacial (but in fact susceptible) Lady Adeline; the innocent, delicate Aurora Raby; and the 'frolic' Duchess of Fitz-Fulke. Just as events are growing serious with the appearance of 'her frolic Grace' in Juan's bedroom, the story breaks off. Byron departed for the Greek War of Independence and the poem was left incomplete. Yet even allowing for this disadvantage it seems strange that *Don Juan*, X to XVI, has not aroused more enthusiasm.

In these final cantos Byron completed his revitalisation of

Popean satire. In the earlier cantos of the poem the satire had been angled obliquely at the English through contrasts with Continental ways and values. Now at last the scene becomes England and the English are allowed to enact their own failings and foibles in their natural setting. By placing his characters within a closely-observed, socially accurate context, Byron is able to let them throw ironic highlights on themselves and one another through the contrasts which they create. When such contrast is faint, or when special emphasis is required, Byron's narrator figure does not hesitate to supply it:

> But how shall I relate in other cantos
> Of what befell our hero in the land,
> Which 'tis the common cry and lie to vaunt as
> A moral country? But I hold my hand—
> For I disdain to write an Atalantis;
> But 'tis as well at once to understand,
> You are *not* a moral people, and you know it,
> Without the aid of too sincere a poet.
> (*Don Juan*, XI. lxxxvii)

Byron's obvious predecessor in this kind of realistic moral storytelling (even down to the use of extensive authorial comment) was Fielding. And as in Fielding the use of literary burlesque and parody (which had carried so much of the weight of ironic contrast in the earlier cantos) now becomes submerged and muted. The satire on England no longer needs these contrasts from without, supplied by plot and literary parody: the characters can be made to do all that is necessary from within. In these last cantos of *Don Juan* Byron developed a whole new technique for the dramatisation of aristocratic snobberies, political and financial manipulations and the sexual tensions and mischief set up by the enforced idleness of the womenfolk. He brought Fielding's social comedy up to date, going far beyond the range of the serious novelists of his generation (including Peacock, of whose comic writing he appears to have had some knowledge) and beats into the ground in terms of real aristocratic attitudes and elegance the minor fashionable novelists of the contemporary 'Silver fork' school. The truthfulness of Byron's picture can be checked against the letters and diaries of his contemporaries (or indeed his own). His superior grasp of the basic energies which impelled that society provide the way forward from Fielding and Smollett to Thackeray and Trollope in the age which followed his.

In another sense too the comparison of the English cantos of *Don Juan* with Byron's letters and journals may prove helpful. As Byron advances into *Don Juan* the gap between his flexibility, immediacy and range as a prose writer and the qualities of his poetry narrows, and by the time he is well into the poem and writing *The Vision of Judgment* it has virtually disappeared. *The Vision of Judgment* itself may be instanced, indeed, as bringing together all the qualities that have been under discussion. In it Byron works up his scathing detestation of postwar England and its governing classes ('this scene of royal itch and loyal scratching' (*Don Juan*, XI. lxxviii)), which has been gaining increasingly strong expression in both his letters and *Don Juan*, into a poem of Popean strength and resonance. His comment on the funeral of the blind, deaf, mad and aged George III sums up much of what the poem has to say in an image of Popean vividness and Johnsonian weight (and justice):

> And when the gorgeous coffin was laid low,
> It seemed the mockery of hell to fold
> The rottenness of eighty years in gold.
> (*Vision of Judgment*, x)

This 'rottenness of eighty years' is not only the rottenness of the royal corpse but also the archaic, corrupted political structure which is his reign's legacy. In *The Vision of Judgment* images open outwards (as in Pope) to reveal greater areas of satirical relevance. And the structure of the poem is at one with this. It began as a travesty of Robert Southey's official ode on the death of the old king (Byron's regular target being now Poet Laureate), and in the true Augustan manner of literary burlesque it keeps close to the form of its original while ceaselessly pouring scorn on it. Southey's stately scene at Heaven's gate, where notable blessed spirits advance to sing the monarch's praises before he is wafted into Paradise, turns into an undignified dispute over the destiny of the royal soul, which is only solved when one of the devils arrives with Southey under his wing and the Laureate's funeral ode throws all parties into an equal state of confusion:

> Those grand heroics acted as a spell;
> The Angels stopped their ears and plied their pinions;
> The Devils ran howling, deafened, down to Hell;
> The ghosts fled, gibbering, for their own dominions—
> (For 'tis not yet decided where they dwell,
> And I leave every man to his opinions);
> Michael took refuge in his trump—but, lo!
> His teeth were set on edge, he could not blow!
>
> (*Vision of Judgment*, ciii)

At which point George III slips into Heaven amid the confusion and is last seen 'practising the hundredth psalm' ('Enter into his gates with thanksgiving, and into his courts with praise ... for the Lord is good; his mercy everlasting.')

Byron has all the resources of the eighteenth-century satirist at his fingertips in *The Vision of Judgment* and he is now completely in command. The poem uses tradition for its own purposes, ranging from farcical travesty to grand Miltonic imitation which opens up the relevance of the tale from the purely local and English into a universal allegory of dignity and grubby-mindedness. And in this last area Byron is still free to carry off breathtakingly rapid, stinging insults of the kind we have already seen in the best parts of *English Bards, and Scotch Reviewers*. Yet now the insults are more resonant, because Southey stands displayed as the emblem of all *Dunciad* writers that have ever written:

> He had sung against all battles, and again
> In their high praise and glory; he had called
> Reviewing 'the ungentle craft,' and then
> Became as base a critic as e'er crawled—
> Fed, paid, and pampered by the very men
> By whom his muse and morals had been mauled:

> He had written much blank verse, and blanker prose,
> And more of both than any body knows.
>
> (*Vision of Judgment*, xcviii)

The English cantos of *Don Juan* are equally rich in satirical relevance, their literary echoes equally resonant. Even when the tone is at its lightest one finds that images or assertions work in two directions at once: downward towards their roots in a closely-observed sociological study of society and its make-up; upwards in a sparkle of literary associations and evocations which links Byron with the satire of his contemporaries. For example, the catalogue of guests at Norman Abbey, the country house to which Juan goes after the fatigues of the London season, includes the following vignette:

> There were the six Miss Rawbolds—pretty dears!
> All song and sentiment; whose hearts were set
> Less on a convent than a coronet.
>
> (*Don Juan*, XIII. lxxxv)

The mockery is conventional, but it belongs to a current convention (as witness the young ladies from the boarding school with their harp and refinements who grace Jane Austen's *Sanditon*), while beneath the surface Byron's constant concern to define the springs of social energy and identify its perversion of surface 'reality' is as hard at work as usual ('pretty dears!/All song and sentiment. . . set/Less on a convent than a coronet'). Furthermore, besides the literary mockery of affectation there is also the mockery of affected literature in the passing shot at the 'convent and coronet' school with its sentimentalised pictures of young womanhood.

Many critics have objected to the loose narrative structure of the later cantos of *Don Juan*, instancing the fact that after half a dozen cantos Byron has scarcely got his love-intrigue going. But in fact the second part of the poem shows ample signs of organisation. Byron was now so thoroughly in command of his materials that he often wrote a canto in under a fortnight, yet Canto XI (written in the same number of days) is tightly enough knit to balance Don Juan's arrival in lamplit commercial London (xxii, one quarter of the way through) with his progress into the glare of the lamps in the fashionable squares (lxvii, the three-quarter point). This balancing of the two great sources of power in Regency London recalls the structural formality of Pope, but as in the best of Pope it is so unobtrusively assimilated into the larger purpose of the poem at this moment (suggesting the energy, rush and self-confidence of the Regency metropolis) as to pass almost unnoticed.

For the most part the later cantos of *Don Juan* are unified by means which plainly show how Byron had succeeded in revitalising the traditions with which he was working. Recurring images, satirical points, jokes serve to bind events together, while the transformations worked on them at each reappearance show Byron's up-to-date, evolutionary handling of them. For example, when Juan first lands in England he is staggered by the hotel bills at Dover:

> Thy cliffs, *dear* Dover! harbour, and hotel;
> Thy custom-house, with all its delicate duties;
> Thy waiters running mucks at every bell . . .
> And last, not least, to strangers uninstructed,
> Thy long, long bills, whence nothing is deducted.
> (*Don Juan*, X. lxix)

In the following canto Juan is attacked by footpads on Shooter's Hill, kills one in self-defence and then pauses, as a bewildered foreigner with an overwhelming sense of the strangeness of all things English, to wonder what it was all about:

> 'Perhaps,' thought he, 'it is the country's wont
> To welcome foreigners in this way: now
> I recollect some innkeepers who don't
> Differ, except in robbing with a bow,
> In lieu of a bare blade and brazen front.'
> (*Don Juan*, XI. xv)

The Dover joke is here picked up and given a fresh satiric twist. A few stanzas later, when Juan arrives at St James's and enters his hotel, Byron lets the joke echo once again. His attention is now on other things, but the joke can still be slipped in: it prolongs the satirical effect and helps unify the picture of Juan's experiences. Juan advances

> Into one of the sweetest of hotels,
> Especially for foreigners—and mostly
> For those whom favour or whom fortune swells,
> And cannot find a bill's small items costly.
> (*Don Juan*, XI. xxxi)

By means such as this Byron unifies the surface of his story and its running commentary of satire. It is a forward-moving unity, well-suited to a narrative with many of the characteristics of a novel. The edge and the imagination of Popean satire are preserved, but with the necessary Romantic dynamic movement. And in one further respect Byron revitalises his models and sources.

The novelist/commentator of Fielding's works fuses with Sterne's mocking sentimentalist in *Don Juan*. In the earlier European and Turkish cantos he satirises from the outside. In the English ones he re-enters his society, draws closer to the characters he has created and satirises from within. The storyteller's voice ranges the whole gamut from Fielding:

> But now I'm going to be immoral; now
> I mean to show things really as they are,
> Not as they ought to be
> (*Don Juan*, XII. xl)

or Swift:

> The black loam long manured by Vice
> (*Don Juan*, XII. xl)

to Sternian wilfulness:

> But now I will begin my poem. 'Tis
> Perhaps a little strange, if not quite new,
> That from the first of Cantos up to this
> I've not begun what we have to go through.
> These first twelve books are merely flourishes,
> *Preludios*, trying just a string or two
> Upon my lyre, or making the pegs sure;
> And when so, you shall have the overture.
>
> (*Don Juan*, XII.liv)

Sentiment too, and full personal revelation are possible and the entire range and brilliance of Byron's conversation in his letters are faithfully reproduced. Meanwhile the story-telling, as such, is of equal range and diversity.

It seems impossible to do justice to the full power of Byron's satirical achievement in his last works. Perhaps the only conclusion likely to suggest the distance he had covered in integrating his poetic with his prose-writing self and the way he had revitalised poetic satire in the process, making it once again a living genre, fully capable of dealing with Regency folly and pretence, is a final comparison between those stiff early satires and *Don Juan*. In *The Waltz* there is a passage about a fashionable dance in which (characteristically) first-hand observation gets lost beneath the conventionalities of the heroic couplet:

> The Ball begins—the honours of the house
> First duly done by daughter or by spouse,
> Some Potentate—or royal or serene—
> With Kent's gay grace, or sapient Gloster's mien,
> Leads forth the ready dame, whose rising flush
> Might once have been mistaken for a blush.
>
> (*The Waltz*, ll. 184-9)

In *Don Juan*, XI, the daughter or spouse who is rather vaguely set to do the honours gloriously expands and becomes the central victim of the animated, fashionable scene. That the 'potentates' should have been deprived of their leading place in the dance and condemned, like Regency Sisyphus figures, to a never-ending, pointless, effortful climb, only stresses Byron's gain as an artist and an observer in the ten years which separate the two pieces:

> There stands the noble hostess, nor shall sink
> With the three-thousandth curtsy; there the waltz,
> The only dance which teaches girls to think,
> Makes one in love even with its very faults.
> Saloon, room, hall, o'erflow beyond their brink,
> And long the latest of arrivals halts,
> 'Midst royal dukes and dames condemned to climb,
> And gain an inch of staircase at a time.
> <div align="right">(<i>Don Juan</i>, XI. lxviii)</div>

8 'A LIGHT TO LESSON AGES': BYRON'S POLITICAL PLAYS

Anne Barton

In September 1821 Byron sent John Murray the manuscript of a rhapsody in three acts, 'in my gay metaphysical style'. To Thomas Moore he confided in a letter of 19 September that *Cain* was to be subtitled *A Mystery*, 'according to the former Christian custom, and in honour of what it probably will remain to the reader'. Like most of Byron's jokes, this one about the impenetrability of *Cain* was fundamentally serious. Although *Manfred*, a dramatic poem which approximated to a familiar Gothic mode, developing attitudes already made popular by *Childe Harold* and the verse tales, was praised and on the whole comprehended in its own time, Byron's seven other plays – with the significant exception of *Werner* – proved thorny and baffling from the start. In this same September he confessed to Murray that Gifford's adverse criticism of *The Two Foscari* and *Sardanapalus* had wounded him: 'to be sure, they are as opposite to the English drama as one thing can be to another; but I have a notion that, if understood, they will in time find favour (though *not* on the stage) with the reader.' Byron did not often appeal in this way to 'the Avenger, Time' to vindicate literary works which his contemporaries had misprized or misunderstood. He was all too aware that Time is an unreliable legatee, that posterity 'does not often claim the bright reversion' (*Don Juan*, Dedication, ix). Posterity has, in fact, recognised the integrity and brilliance of *Don Juan*, as Byron wistfully hoped it might. The plays, on the other hand, despite some perceptive twentieth-century criticism, are still waiting to come into their own.

Werner, Byron's one genuinely bad and derivative play, was also his one indisputable theatrical success. A kind of shoddy As You

Like It, indulging without examining the tastes and fantasies of its nineteenth-century audience, this farrago of murder, remorse, mouldering castle halls, secret passages, honour, improbable deception and disguise held the stage almost without a break between 1830 and 1861. Macready, Phelps and Irving all triumphed in it.[1] Although Byron published *Werner* in 1822 with the usual caveat ('neither intended, nor in any shape adapted, for the stage') this declaration, as the theatre itself was quick to recognise, was simply not true. Byron began *Werner* in 1815, while he was helping to manage Drury Lane, and the play was designed specifically for that theatre. He had not quite completed the first act when 'Lady Byron's farce put it out of my head for the time of her representation' (to Murray, 9 October 1821) but when he returned to the project six years later he lapsed back without difficulty into the old popular mode. There is nothing remarkable about *Werner*, except the fact that Byron should have bothered to take it up again after *Marino Faliero, The Two Foscari, Sardanapalus* and *Cain*.

David Erdman has argued convincingly that, for all his passionate disclaimers, Byron did have hopes that *Marino Faliero, The Two Foscari* and *Sardanapalus* might be acted.[2] It was, as Erdman points out, during the period when Byron mistakenly believed that *Marino Faliero*, in spite of protests by author and publisher, not to mention the Lord Chancellor's injunction, had been a success at Drury Lane, that he rapidly completed his other two regular tragedies. When the truth finally reached Ravenna, that *Marino Faliero* had closed after only seven performances to sparse houses, Byron immediately scrapped his plans for the tragedies of Tiberius and Francesca da Rimini and turned instead to the composition of Biblical drama of a kind that no one, as he believed, could even attempt to act. It was really Byron's touchiness, his morbid fear of failure, which led him to guard tragedies which he could openly refer to as 'experiments' or 'reforms' against the terrible risk of performance. If only *Marino Faliero* had succeeded — and Byron's delight when he thought it had is unmistakable — he would have settled happily into his new role as a practising playwright with a mission to revitalise and transform the contemporary stage.

For a man who once declared that he would never willingly

have anything to do with the theatres, Byron spent a surprising amount of time in them, whether as a member of the Drury Lane Sub-Committee, backstage, or merely as a playgoer. A talented amateur actor himself, he could be powerfully moved by what he saw on the stage. His response to Kean's performance as Sir Giles Overreach in Massinger's *A New Way To Pay Old Debts* was so violent that it brought on a species of convulsive fit. His emotions got the better of him again, a few years later, during a performance of Alfieri's tragedy *Mirra*. Byron was vulnerable to great acting, especially in plays which seemed to touch upon and heighten his own personal dilemmas. Nevertheless he was more acutely and intelligently aware than any of the other Romantics of exactly what was wrong with the contemporary London stage, of the extent to which it had deadened and degraded itself and could only be rescued now by the most radical reforms. Even after a nervous management had excised the lines attacking the current fashion for real horses and other purely spectacular devices,[3] Byron's 'Address, Spoken At The Opening Of Drury Lane Theatre' on 10 October 1812 is still remarkable for its celebration of the vanished glory of the English theatre, and the pessimism with which it regards 'the sinking stage' of recent years – a stage which 'could condescend / To soothe the sickly taste it dare not mend'. Compared to the praise showered upon the memory of Shakespeare, Garrick and Mrs Siddons, Byron's hope for the revived Drury Lane, 'All past reproach may present scenes refute', seems curiously, and prophetically, hollow.

There are almost too many reasons for the gradual cheapening and decline of the English stage in the eighteenth and nineteenth centuries: sentimentalism and prudery, the siphoning off of creative energy into the novel, the changing composition of the audience, the establishment of tyrannical stage conventions which debased drama and, above all, the sense that a great tradition had exhausted itself without appointing an heir. Without exception the major Romantic poets all believed in the idea of the theatre: indeed, they tended to regard a flourishing drama as evidence of the health of society. Wordsworth, Coleridge, Shelley and Keats all wrote at least one tragedy for the stage. Minor poets deluged the playhouses with their offerings. When Byron took up his post at Drury Lane he was staggered by the number of manuscripts submitted and, after reading them, by their almost unrelieved badness: 'There never were such things as most of them' ('Detached Thoughts', 67).

In general, the plays of the early nineteenth century were parasitic either upon the Gothic novel, producing vast, sprawling Germanic dramas of ghosts and ruined castles, incest and vengeance, or upon Shakespeare: 'the worst of models', as Byron pointed out, 'though the most extraordinary of writers' (to Murray, 14 July 1821). There was little to choose between the Gothic mode and the bastard-Elizabethan. Both resulted in plays that were profoundly subjective, sentimental, more lyrical than dramatic, and geared to the star actor. It was the purpose of the evening to tear a passion, or the audience's sympathies, to tatters. Overwrought, sensational and self-indulgent, the theatre of Byron's time was resolutely escapist. It was very much concerned to hint at something nasty in the woodshed, but the woodshed itself was almost invariably mullioned and triple-arched and haunted by what Sheridan, in *The Critic*, described as the heroine stark mad in white satin, and her confidante stark mad in white linen. In a time of general social turmoil, when England hovered on the brink of revolution, when the country was agonising toward the Reform Bill of 1832, when Catholic emancipation, the misery of the working classes confronting the Industrial Revolution, the problem of the suffrage and (for a good many years) the threat of Napoleon, were all convulsing society, the theatre went on raising mediaeval ghosts, exploring the delicious fears of maidens captive in towers, precipitating villains through trap doors, and maundering on about the noble race of Siegendorff unhappily, and guiltily, extinct. It was completely cut off from the political, social and emotional world of its audience, let alone from the situation of England as a whole. People went to Drury Lane to buy a few hours of oblivion, to empathise with Mr Kean being passionate in some extraordinary situation, and generally to abdicate as rational human beings. Joyously hypnotised by the play, the acting and the stage spectacle, they were able 'to swap a contradictory world for a consistent one,

one that they scarcely know for one of which they can dream'.[4] The words are those of Bertolt Brecht, writing in *A Short Organum For the Theatre* (1948) about his own struggle to persuade audiences and actors to *think* in the playhouse. Any imaginary meeting that one can project between Byron and Brecht is potentially explosive. Yet the two men would, in certain important ways, have understood one another. Certainly Brecht more than anyone else has helped to create a twentieth-century theatre in which Byron's political plays might, at last, find a public.

Marino Faliero, The Two Foscari and *Sardanapalus* never enjoyed the quasi-permanent status in the repertory achieved for a time by *Werner*. What theatrical success they have had was due not to any understanding of the works themselves and how to stage them but simply to the fact that through drastic cutting, various alterations and 'improvements', and the strenuous efforts of leading actors, they could be transformed into mindless spectacles. When Byron congratulated himself on the fact that a strictly regular drama must escape travesty on the stage because it deprived actors of any opportunity for 'tossing their heads and kicking their heels' (Diary, 12 January 1821), he did not foresee the live horses, full *corps de ballet*, carefully researched Assyrian costumes, real water gurgling through Canaletto's Venice, and the symphony orchestras (not to mention the city of Nineveh by sunset, twilight, moonlight, and finally in flames) under which his finely reasoned political plays were going to be buried alive. It was as though *Mother Courage* had first been presented to the world in a film version by Cecil B. de Mille.

From the very beginning the literary reviews of Byron's historical plays tended to reflect the nature and prejudices of that contemporary theatre from which he was attempting to break away. He was castigated for not achieving emotional effects which, like Brecht after him, he had specifically tried to avoid. Hazlitt, reviewing *Marino Faliero*, complained that Byron seemed unable to take an historical event, transport us to the time and place of action, give us a real, living interest in the same, and by filling the mind with the agonizing hopes, and panic-fears, and incorrigible will, and sudden projects of the authentic actors in the world's volume, charm us out of ourselves ... Lord Byron's page has not this effect; it is modern, smooth, fresh from Mr. Murray's, and does not smack of the olden time. It is not rough, Gothic, pregnant with past events, unacquainted with the present time ... The author does not try to make us *overhear* what old Faliero, and his young wife, and his wily, infuriated accomplices would say, but makes them his proxies to discuss the topics of love and marriage, the claims of rank and common justice ... *Marino Faliero* is without a plot, without characters, without fluctuating interest, and without the spirit of dialogue.[5]

Jeffrey, in an unsigned notice in the *Edinburgh Review*, expressed himself as wholly perplexed by Byron's choice in *Marino Faliero* of a story 'without love or hatred – misanthropy or pity – containing nothing voluptuous and nothing terrific – but depending, for its grandeur, on the anger of a very old and irritable man.'[6] Drama, he argued, should steer clear of 'abstract deductions of reason', and he concluded that 'if, in setting down a vehement invective [Byron] does not fancy the tone in which Mr. Kean would deliver it, and anticipate the long applauses of the pit, then he may be sure that neither his feelings nor his genius are in unison with the stage at all'.

Jeffrey was not alone in finding the subject of *Marino Faliero* undramatic. The opinion was commonly voiced. Another reviewer asserted that, even if historically true, the idea of a man feeling resentment as powerful as that of the Doge for a cause so trivial was basically improbable: and so 'no more fitting a subject for a poet than an animal with two heads would be for an artist of a different description'.[7] To believe, of course, that Byron's Faliero conspires to overthrow his own class in Venice only, or even principally, because of Steno's ribald jest, is grossly to misread the play: to simplify what the dramatist has made complex. The fact that the criticism could be made at all, especially considering the wild psychological improbability of most Gothic tragedy, is, however, a measure of the extent to which Byron's contemporaries had been conditioned by the theatre of their own time in their attitude towards motivation in drama. There was similar difficulty over the objective correlative in *The Two Foscari* and *Sardanapalus*.

Marino Faliero was often compared unfavourably with Otway's *Venice Preserv'd* (1682). Byron himself liked Otway's play – 'all except of that maudlin bitch of chaste lewdness and blubbering curiosity, Belvidera, whom I utterly despise, abhor and detest' – but he considered the story of Faliero, simply as a story, to be so much finer a tragic plot that he told Murray, even before he had begun his own play, that Otway should have chosen it instead (2 April 1817). This judgement, which Byron's contemporaries regarded as merely eccentric, was shrewd. *Venice Preserv'd* is limited by the fact that it is essentially a domestic tragedy. A play about the rivalry between love and friendship, both of them carried to an overwrought and pathetic extreme, it comes closest to being genuinely political in the notorious Nicky-Nacky scenes involving the alleged sexual tastes of the Earl of Shaftesbury. The conspiracy itself is little more than an excuse for manoeuvring Jaffeir, his wife Belvidera, and his friend Pierre into the most heartrending series of private imbroglios that Otway could devise. The last thing that this dramatist wanted his audience or readers to do – at least in his tragedies; the comedies are a very different matter – was to think, not only because if they did they might stop crying, but because *Venice Preserv'd* simply will not stand up under any genuine application of reason. Decline for an instant to be swept away, to be hypnotised by the plangent softness and excess of Otway's verse, and the supposedly admirable Belvidera becomes just what Byron said she was, a maudlin bitch, and even Pierre and the tearful Jaffeir singularly literary and unlikely. Love leads both men to plot against the state, love for a wife in Jaffeir's case, for a courtesan in that of Pierre. When, in Act Three, Otway compares Jaffeir with Brutus and Belvidera with Portia, the tremendous memory of Shakespeare and of concerns which in *Julius Caesar* were genuine, but have here become mere window dressing, comes close to demolishing his play.

Byron invokes Brutus and Caesar on a number of occasions in *Marino Faliero*, but this identification of a Venetian present with a Roman past is purposeful in ways that make it seem as though Byron's play were engaged in a dialogue with Shakespeare's, as though *Marino Faliero* were a sequel to *Julius Caesar* in a different mode. Just before his execution, the Doge muses on the fact that the two popular leaders, 'the plebeian Brutus' and 'the quick Cassius of the Arsenal' have preceded him in death. At this moment Faliero sees the hot-tempered and relentless Philip Calendaro in the role of Cassius, Israel Bertuccio as Brutus. Bertuccio, however, made his first appearance in the play in the role of Cassius. He was the original and cunning tempter who played upon the accumulated discontents of the Doge, seducing him with the idea that he might become true sovereign lord of a free and happy people. Faliero himself is associated with Brutus (with all the ambiguity of motive and the self-torment that implies), but it is impossible to forget that his position in the state, at least nominally, is that of Caesar. Throughout the play, Byron's use of Shakespearean reference is riddling and intellectually provocative. It is not a simple device for bestowing importance upon his characters.

Like *Julius Caesar, Marino Faliero* is about revolution and the relationship between personal feelings and public causes. It is something *Venice Preserv'd* was not: a political play. Byron meditated the subject for several years before embarking on it, and he prided himself, characteristically, on his fidelity to historical fact. When, after the tragedy had already been sent to Murray, he stumbled upon an early manuscript life of Faliero, he was delighted to find that his conception of the character was fundamentally correct, that he had divined how the real Faliero had behaved and spoken at a number of points. He was especially pleased to discover that his rejection of jealousy as a motive, a rejection made both on artistic grounds – because jealousy seemed to him an exhausted topic of drama – and because he felt instinctively that it did not accord with the character of Faliero, was historically accurate.

Most of the energy of Byron's first historical tragedy derives from the Doge. In the sultry world of the play, a world of sirocco, overcast skies, and a dull moon, his frustration and unrest drive events along. This is not, however, a part which Kean or any of the other star actors of Byron's day could find really attractive. Faliero is not only an old man, verging on eighty; there is nothing romantic about him, or about his relationship with his young and decidedly frosty wife Angiolina. Byron has handled the character in such a way as to prevent the audience from identifying with him. We are forced to stand back from the Doge, to observe and analyse without pretending to share his experience. The situation in Venice seems, as a result, less like that nostalgic page from 'the olden time' that Hazlitt required than a reality involving one's own contemporary choices and beliefs. *Marino Faliero* helps to explain what Byron meant when he described his plays as 'mental theatre' (to Murray, 23 August 1821). They are not merely, or even primarily, closet drama, but plays designed to make an audience think.

In believing that Faliero conspired to overthrow the state because Michael Steno ornamented the ducal throne with some obscene graffiti touching upon the nature of his marriage, and escaped virtually without punishment, reviewers ignored the facts of Byron's tragedy. As the Doge knows, Steno's insult was only 'the last drop / Which makes the cup run o'er, and mine was full / Already' (v.i.245–7). Byron's Faliero is an intensely lonely man who, for some time before the play opens, has been nursing an accumulation of grievances against his own class. These grievances are a subtle mixture of the personal and the public, the selfish and the disinterested. Faliero himself finds it difficult to separate political idealism from wounded pride and, because he is a desperately honest man, this uncertainty about the extent to which the springs of his own actions are contaminated increases his agony of spirit. His concern for the plight of the Venetian people under patrician tyranny is genuine and long-standing. Although he does dream at the beginning of the play, with the help of both Bertuccio's, of a democracy which he himself would rule as elected king, he comes to see that this ambition is tainted and corrupt: 'I will resign a crown, and make the state / Renew its freedom' (IV.ii.159–60).

The renunciation is important because, as the Doge is aware, his hatred of the patricians is based not only upon their treatment of the people, but their mockery of his own high office. They made him Doge in his absence, without informing him that they had just altered the statutes of Venice so as to strip the position of any real power. Then these old friends and comrades of his youth and maturity withdrew from him. They severed all social ties and left him enthroned, like a statue of himself, in splendid isolation.

There is no one in the play to whom the Doge can really talk. His nephew Bertuccio Faliero is loyal, but essentially uncomprehending. For him, the obvious course to adopt once the Forty have refused to punish Steno would be the time-honoured one of private revenge: a knife in the dark, followed by a discreet splash in the canal, and there an end. The Doge's refusal to have this done perplexes him, and although he falls in with the conspiracy, there is a strong sense that he does so out of traditional family loyalty and with only the most confused grasp of the issues actually involved. The Doge does come to respect Calendaro and Israel Bertuccio, the two chief plotters. Significantly, the fact that Bertuccio once served under him as a soldier, that he was there at Zara, and so belongs to Faliero's vanished world of comradeship and heroic endeavour, makes it easier to effect a *rapprochement*. And yet, at the age of almost fourscore, the Doge cannot really cease to be a patrician. Not only does he find it impossible to forget that, whatever their crimes, the high-born men he proposes to butcher were once his friends and shared his life; he is obsessed with his own ancestry, with the indignity of making one with 'stung plebeians'. Although he knows that the misery of the people cries out for redress, he still dreads (even as Byron did himself) the possibility and characteristics of popular rule: 'for what is (*in fact*) democracy? an Aristocracy of Blackguards' ('My Dictionary', May 1821). It is characteristic of both Faliero and his creator that, in the tense moments before the great bell of St Mark's sounds, the Doge should distrust the temper of the citizens and wish that rebellion lay in the hands of his own, trusty feudal retainers on his country estate: men who would obey his orders unquestioningly, like his nephew, or his soldiers of the past. This is not the attitude of a convinced republican.

Angiolina, Faliero's young wife, has almost invariably been regarded as an absolute in the play, an unexamined if unenticing ideal, but it is hard to believe that this is what Byron intended. His own dislike of 'chilly women', exacerbated by his mistake in actually marrying one, was lifelong, and Angiolina is a perfect refrigerator. Byron may well have been reacting against Otway's tearful Belvidera when he created her, but her attitudes and point of view are presented none the less as limited. She is right when, at the beginning of the play, she urges her husband to forget about Steno's 'absurd lampoon', when she claims that a severe sentence passed against this 'false and flippant libeller' would only magnify the importance of his deed. Controlled, rational, strong-willed and extremely conservative, Angiolina functions immaculately within the limits of that aristocratic code of female duty to which she has been bred. The code, however, has its deficiencies. When a rash friend inquires whether she has never had any natural regrets at marrying a man three times her age simply because it was her dying father's wish, Angiolina's rebuke causes ice crystals to form in the room:

> I feel no wrath, but some surprise: I knew not
> That wedded bosoms could permit themselves
> To ponder upon what they *now* might choose,
> Or aught save their past choice.
>
> (II.i.126–9)

As with Desdemona's childlike incredulity when Emilia indicates that there are unfaithful wives in the world, Angiolina's 'surprise' suggests that there are other reasons, apart from disparity in age, why her husband is not open with her.

Angiolina cannot play Portia to Faliero's Brutus, and the failure matters. Locked as she is within a set of rigid social and moral certainties which she never questions, it does not occur to her even at the end that Faliero might have acted as he did for reasons more complicated and less personal than Steno's insult. In her imagination, as in that of Byron's reviewers, it was only 'Steno's lie, couch'd in two worthless lines' which 'put in peril / A senate which hath stood eight hundred years' (v.i.444–6). Angiolina remembers that Troy, Rome and Christian Spain all met their downfall because of a woman. Her conviction that Venice has only just escaped the same fate – 'And I have been the cause, the unconscious cause' (v.ii.7) – is not only overstated but naively self-congratulatory. From it she extracts her own refusal to pardon Steno when he humbly asks her forgiveness in the last scene, or even to address him directly. A staunch defender of the political *status quo*, she passes precisely that clear judgement on Faliero that the play as a whole argues is impossible. 'Thou hast been guilty', she tells him severely, 'of a great offence' (v.i.382).

Angiolina's assessment of her husband's actions is clearly inadequate, but Byron refuses to sketch out any clear-cut and acceptable alternative. There is no easy answer to the problem of Faliero's innocence or guilt, the mingled grandeur and pettiness of his behaviour, because in real life there are no easy answers to the issues this play sets out to explore. The human mind tends to be divided against itself, as Faliero knows only too bitterly: 'Like the demon who believes and trembles / Must I abhor and do' (III.ii.520–1). Even while he tries to argue his way out of the predicament, his own words betray him to himself:

> injured souls
> Oft do a public right with private wrong,
> And justify their deeds unto themselves.
> (IV.ii.105–7)

The Doge may be old and arrogant; he is too intelligent not to understand and writhe under a situation in which he finds himself hating the patricians 'doubly for the deeds / Which I must do to pay them back for theirs' (III.i.116–17). When Philip Calendaro promises that he will present the Doge with the head of Steno, as an act of personal homage, after the massacre is over, Faliero repulses the offer with something like panic. He can see its implications all too clearly.

It is true that the Doge has moments of self-deception, of

desperate sophistry in which he tries to pretend that the senators 'have no *private* life, / Nor claim to ties they have cut off from others' (III.ii.382), or that 'the blood of tyrants is not human' (IV.ii.163). Shakespeare's Brutus had asserted, in much the same manner, that 'in the spirit of men there is no blood' – and then found that the sheer physical mess created by the assassination was so great that extreme measures were required in order to preserve the fiction of a ritual act: 'Stoop, Romans, stoop, / And let us bathe our hands in Caesar's blood'. At this moment, and indeed throughout the play, Brutus is confident of the approbation of posterity. Byron's Faliero is both more self-aware and more cynical. He is stingingly conscious, not only of the way he can lie to himself, but of the fact that history will judge him not according to the honesty of his dealings or the justice of his cause, but simply on the amoral basis of failure or success. The calumnies of time 'never spare the fame of him who fails, / But try the Caesar, or the Catiline, / By the true touchstone of desert – success' (I.ii.594–6).

In the end, revolution fails in Venice. The people remain enslaved by the aristocracy, Bertuccio and Philip Calendaro are tortured, gagged lest they speak to the crowd, then executed, and the Doge is not only beheaded but his memory expunged from the annals of the city he loved, all because one of the conspirators, Bertram, cannot bear that a man who is more a childhood memory than a real friend should share the general fate. When Bertram tries to warn Lioni not to attend the Council at dawn with the other patricians, Lioni's suspicions are aroused. He plays upon Bertram's personal feelings, extracts the truth, and immediately reveals it to the Forty. Byron handles Lioni brilliantly. His long soliloquy in Act Four, after he has returned home early, obscurely troubled, from a ball which represents at once the corruption of the Venetian aristocracy and the splendour of the civilisation it has created, is no mere poetic self-indulgence, an undramatic hymn in praise of the Grand Canal at night. Lioni is allowed to tell us what and how he perceives, how complex and sensitive his awareness is of selected aspects of the world he inhabits, in order that it should be clear what kind of loss is involved in deciding to obliterate a human consciousness like this one.

Because Bertram's personal feelings triumph over his political convictions, Lioni escapes death. It will be the different personalities and modes of apprehension of other friends – Bertuccio and Calendaro – which are sacrificed. Whether there is a revolution in Venice, or there is not, pain and waste seem to be inevitable. Which course, then, is better? If Byron, in the play as in his own life, ultimately tips the balance on the side of revolution, *Marino Faliero* is none the less not Brecht's *Days of the Commune*: a straightforward, didactic counsel to harden one's heart for the sake of the cause. The play simply presents the facts of the matter as honestly and as fully as it can. If men set out to overthrow an otherwise unassailable tyranny by violence, they must be prepared to trample on their human instincts and emotional ties, to falsify their own natures and mythologise those of their victims. The need to make or avoid this decision seems to be constant. In Venice, in the year 1355, this is what certain historical individuals, the products of a particular place, time and situation, did when faced with it.

The Two Foscari, Byron's second Venetian tragedy, was written in a single creative burst. One way and another, *Marino Faliero* had occupied him for over four years: *The Two Foscari* was conceived and executed in a month. It lacks, as a result, the verbal richness, that dense, metaphoric and symbolic texture (so brilliantly analysed by G. Wilson Knight) of the earlier play. It is possible, remembering Byron's delusion at this time that *Marino Faliero* had succeeded at Drury Lane, that *The Two Foscari* is as spare and stripped down as it is because Byron was allowing himself to think of it specifically as a stage play. Certainly it is far less rhetorical, conceived much less in terms of formal, poetic outbursts, than either of the other two historical tragedies. Apart from one long speech by the old Foscari in Act Two, and two crucial soliloquies given to Jacopo his son, the play unfolds by way of passionate but relatively brief interchanges among, in effect, only six characters.

In all three of his historical tragedies, Byron employed the unities as a way of keeping the seductive but dangerous ghost of Shakespeare at bay. None of the Romantics, not even Keats or

Coleridge, was more steeped in the plays than Byron (though he sometimes liked to shock people with pretended irreverence), and the precaution was probably wise. He was quick to learn, however, how to capitalise on the neo-classical structure in order to achieve certain dramatic effects. *Marino Faliero* had interpreted the unity of place quite liberally. The action moved freely about Venice, from the Doge's palace to the piazza dominated by the equestrian statue, to the meeting place of the conspirators, and back again to the palace to await the summons of the great bell. The weather everywhere was sultry and oppressive, a universal miasma hanging over the city, but at least people were able to walk about in it. In *The Two Foscari*, by contrast, Byron interpreted the unity of place almost as strictly as Racine, and created much the same kind of claustrophobic effect that Racine had built up in *Britannicus* and *Bajazet*. In this Venice, it is impossible to get out of the Palace of the Doges, even though the captives may occasionally be allowed to look through its windows, as poor Jacopo Foscari does in the first scene, onto a life of sunshine and normality in the Piazza San Marco outside. The entire tragedy, not just its third act, takes place in a prison. The palace is an image of Hell, of a police state from which the only escape is death. Brilliantly, Byron links this sense of spatial and physical restraint with an excruciating ideal of stoicism and aristocratic self-control.

For both the Foscari, father and son, the crisis comes when they are ordered by a decree of the Council of Ten to leave the palace. Neither can manage to cross the threshold. Both die in the act of trying to depart, the young man in Act Four, the old one in the final moments of the play. There is no foul play involved, or at least not of any indictable kind.[8] The Doge dies because he simply cannot withstand further battering, cannot step dishonoured and humiliated into the fresh air through the doors he entered in triumph years before. No previous Doge has left the palace except as a corpse, and neither does he. The case of his son Jacopo is more complex. Most critics have regarded the character of Jacopo as disastrous, and his passionate desire to stay in Venice, even in prison or under torture, as highly unlikely. The losing battle which Solzhenitsyn fought against being exiled from Russia in 1973 is a reminder that, even in the twentieth century, men may feel like the young Foscari. For Jacopo, even the police state of Venice is preferable to the loneliness of a man cut off from his own society and culture:

> The mind is much, but is not all. The mind
> Hath nerved me to endure the risk of death,
> And torture positive, far worse than death
> (If death be a deep sleep), without a groan ...
> I know if mind may bear us up, or no,
> For I have such, and shown it before men;
> It sinks in solitude: my soul is social.
>   (III.i. 87–90, 107–9)

Although the Ten finally grant his wife permission to accompany him, craftily reserving his children as hostages of the state, Jacopo cannot face the idea of banishment. The effects of the rack and the wheel, together with an essentially aristocratic effort of will like the one Calantha summons up at the end of Ford's *The Broken Heart*, combine to free him from a fate which he regards – and his persecutor Loredano knows this – as worse than death.

Only Byron would have had the impudence to append the epigraph he did to *The Two Foscari*: 'The *father* softens, but the *governor's* resolved'. The line comes from Mr Puff's ridiculous inset play in Sheridan's *The Critic*, where it provokes Mr Dangle in the audience to remark wearily, 'Aye, that antithesis of persons is a most established figure'. Mr Dangle was quite right. The tragic hero torn between mutually exclusive obligations as loving father and as ruler or just judge can be traced back to the *Oresteia* of Aeschylus. Agamemnon shrinks from sacrificing his daughter Iphigenia, but there is no other way of getting the army to Troy. Shakespeare played with the idea in *Titus Andronicus*, and in the parallel predicaments of Gaunt and York as fathers in *Richard II*, but it was the Restoration that hammered it to death, Nat Lee providing an especially scarifying example in *Lucius Junius Brutus* (1680). Byron's epigraph constituted a cheerful and unabashed announcement that he had based his work on a dramatic cliché. He could dare to point this out because *The Two Foscari* in fact transmutes and revitalises this particularly hackneyed form of the debate between the public and the private worlds, even as *Marino Faliero* before it had made the situation of Brutus seem new.

The Two Foscari is, among other things, a revenge play and its villain Loredano has often been compared to Iago. There probably is some Shakespearean influence here, but what matters is that Iago's kind of undeviating, total evil is now much less a personal phenomenon than the result of a political system. There is no evidence that old Foscari killed Loredano's father and uncle because they stood in the way of his ambition, but then evidence under a government like this tends to be a scarce commodity. Foscari claims that he has always acted openly as Doge, but this was demonstrably not the case in his dealings with Carmagnuolo, and the failure of candour there breeds understandable suspicion. Loredano chooses to believe, and in a sense he cannot be blamed for it, that Foscari owes him two lives. He proceeds to even the balance, not in the manner of the traditional Elizabethan revenger acting outside the law, but by means which are rendered more horrible by the fact that legally they are unimpeachable. A political system based upon secrecy, private malice, and the exclusiveness of a corrupt and powerful oligarchy, not only lends itself to machinations like those of Loredano but encourages them. It ought to be destroyed.

Here, as in *Marino Faliero*, revolution lurks outside the doors of the palace in the form of the discontented citizens of Venice, but they are as incapable of forcing their way into the sanctuary of government as the Foscari are of leaving it. Loredano succeeds entirely. Backed by the state, and with the help of his own acute understanding of his victims' psychology, he turns their chief virtues against them: Jacopo's love of his country, the Doge's outmoded code of aristocratic stoicism and honour. Once again a regime which is not only brutal and repressive but hypocritical, triumphs at the end. Unlike Faliero's Angiolina, Jacopo's wife Marina does represent a standard of value in the play. This is why, although her real name was Lucrezia, Byron abandoned his customary fidelity to historical fact and changed it to one suggesting the spiritual marriage of the true Venice with the sea. Marina, however, not only loses her husband; she is unable at the end to prevent the travesty of a state funeral for old Foscari, the man who has been destroyed by the state. Tidiness is important, the perpetuation of pious and face-saving lies, as the Nazis knew when they poisoned General Rommel and then asked his widow a few months later to choose a design for his official memorial.

In his two Venetian plays, Byron was able to do something that his contemporaries, on the whole, could not. He built upon the somewhat embarrassing heritage of Elizabethan drama in much the way that the Elizabethans had themselves: through a dialogue in which one play answers and extends another without imitating its precedecessor. *Julius Caesar*, and to a lesser extent *Coriolanus*, lie behind *Marino Faliero*. Byron admired Ben Jonson because he was 'a Scholar and a Classic' (to Murray, 4 July 1821), and *The Two Foscari* seems to reflect *Sejanus* (1603) as well as Mr Puff's venerable antithesis between the strict governor and the relenting sire. Unlike the other Romantics, Byron could use the great English dramatic tradition without being overwhelmed by it. It is hard to tell if he was being truthful, or merely defensive, when he claimed that he had never read Marlowe's *Dr. Faustus*. What matters is his insistence that his own Faust could not possibly make a compact with the Devil, that at the end he would brush away the agents of Hell like so many blue-bottles and walk into the next world, tormented and self-destroyed, but a free spirit. Wild and woolly and self-indulgent though it is, as Byron well knew, *Manfred* nevertheless achieves a powerful effect by defeating certain expectations generated by the Faust legend in all its earlier forms. Even *Cain* and *Heaven and Earth* reach back to the mystery cycles in more than a joking sense. They are questioning extensions, not so much of Peele's *David and Bethsabe* (1587) or Pordage's deplorable *Herod and Mariamne* (1673) as of the Wakefield Master's *Mactatio Abel* or those half-hearted murmurings against the will of God to be heard in the York and Chester versions of the Flood.

Sardanapalus too is dependent upon archetypes which it invokes and then deliberately transforms. Behind it there stretches the long line of Tudor political moralities, Marlowe's *Edward II*, Shakespeare's Henry VI trilogy, his *Richard II*, and his final shifting of the terms of the argument in *Antony and Cleopatra*. Byron's tragedy picks up once again the immemorial theme of the weak king, effete and pleasure-loving, who neglects his duties for his diversions. Sardanapalus represents for his nobles a sad falling off from a stern and warlike ideal, even as Edward II did for the Mortimers, or Richard II for Northumberland, Ross and Willoughby. The attitudes which this unkingly king adopts towards glory, conquest and fame are as different from those of his savage forebears as those of Henry VI were from his. What is new in the situation is Byron's insistence that Sardanapalus is a tragic hero whose stance is in certain important respects like that of Falstaff and Sancho Panza: comic characters for whom honour is a chimera, and the pleasures of the flesh more desirable than a vain chase after renown. 'Eat, drink, and love; the rest's not worth a fillip' (1.ii.251). These are the verses with which Sardanapalus has commemorated his founding of two cities, and they are the source of considerable embarrassment to the dutiful chroniclers of his decidedly peculiar reign.

Byron said of this Assyrian Akhnaton that he had made him 'as amiable as my poor powers could render him, . . . almost a comic character' (to Murray, 25 May and 22 July 1821). The violation of decorum here is deliberate, but not irresponsible. Like Falstaff, or Sancho Panza, or Brecht's Azdak, Sardanapalus has some unattractive traits. He is indolent. He has abandoned his queen in favour of a series of concubines culminating in Myrrha and, because he cannot bear to witness his wife's unhappiness, he pretends that she no longer exists. He is childishly vain of his personal appearance, and he over-indulges himself in the delights of food, drink, sex and flattery. His weaknesses are obvious, and yet, like those of Shakespeare's Mark Antony, they are also the source of his strength. When Macready altered the play so as to make Sardanapalus appear less narcissistic, flippant and selfish, he was obeying the dictates of a theatre which did not mind if the tragic protagonist was a criminal, but could not endure the idea that he might be something of a fool.[9] Byron insists that Sardanapalus is both fool and hero, comic and tragic, that he and his actions are hard to evaluate in ways that subject the whole concept of the tragic hero as understood in the early nineteenth century to examination.

There is much that is wrong and even ludicrous about the life of Sardanapalus, as his critics within the play, including the two women who love him, justly point out. What none of them perceives is that his rejection of the traditional ideals of Assyria is right, even though he cannot give his revolt a form worthy of the thinking behind it. An enlightened man of peace, warm, intelligent, and fundamentally courageous, Sardanapalus has been condemned by fate to rule over a collection of bloodthirsty militarists. 'The empire *has been* founded', he tells Myrrha with a half-humorous desperation: 'I cannot go on multiplying empires' (I.ii.549–50). Stubbornly, by the force of his own example, he tries to alter the history and character of Assyria, to persuade his subjects to abandon war, conquest, and even the savage pleasures of the hunt, in favour of a simple enjoyment of existence. Whatever a corrupt priesthood may maintain, Sardanapalus himself has no delusions that there is anything but silence beyond the grave, and life is short.

In pursuing this policy, the king makes some mistakes. He is lazy, and he ventures out of his various pleasure domes too infrequently to see how his corrupt officers in fact frustrate his plans for the welfare of the people. His subjects are not, as he would negligently like to believe, all well-fed and free. At the same time, their revolt against him is really based upon incomprehension more than upon social or economic discontent. In material terms they are no worse off under Sardanapalus than under any of his glorious predecessors. What brings them to rise up and overthrow him is the fact that he will not provide them with any myths of war and conquest to compensate for these long-standing injustices and make their lives seem worthwhile. The Assyrians despise his pacifism. They are also alarmed by his casual contempt for organised religion, that other great panacea for the miseries of life on earth. In effect, Sardanapalus has underestimated the force of man's superstition and animal aggression. Because his own attitudes are charitable, rational and disabused, he expects everyone else to share his feelings, without considering that it may be easier to do so in a palace than a hut.

Eventually, Sardanapalus finds that he must put on armour, take up a sword even if it is heavy and hurts his hand, and deal personally with rebellion. He does so reluctantly at first, but discovers in himself an increasing delight in violence which reassures the few followers he has, but fills his own heart with dismay. After his initial success in battle, he dreams that he is sitting, suspended between life and death, at a banquet with Nimrod and Semiramis, the most famous and also the most ruthless killers among his ancestors. At this feast, the wine has turned to blood, and there are other goblets filled with things even worse. Sardanapalus refuses this unholy communion, even as he refused in the waking world to execute Arbaces and the high-priest, the two chief plotters against his throne. He is right, but the decision dooms him. Ironically, Arbaces is so baffled by the clemency of the king that he is easily led to believe it must be a ruse under which Sardanapalus is concealing some truly hideous vengeance. Incapable like everyone else in the play, even Myrrha, of understanding Sardanapalus' ideals, Arbaces sweeps aside his momentary doubt and obediently follows Beleses.

At the end there is nothing for Sardanapalus to do except to make his palace a vast funeral pyre and burn in it himself, his Greek mistress, and all the tangible possessions of a vanished line of kings. As in all of Byron's plays, evil has triumphed. For Sardanapalus himself, the only hope lies in the idea that his story will be transmitted to future times. This is why he arranges for himself a death so spectacular: the glare of this enormous fire will persist in the memories of men,

> Not a mere pillar form'd of cloud and flame
> A beacon in the horizon for a day,
> And then a mount of ashes, but a light
> To lesson ages, rebel nations, and
> Voluptuous princes. Time shall quench full many
> A people's records, and a hero's acts;
> Sweep empire after empire, like this first

> Of empires, into nothing; but even then
> Shall spare this deed of mine, and hold it up
> A problem few dare imitate, and none
> Despise—but, it may be, avoid the life
> Which led to such a consummation.
>
> (v.i.436–49)

Sardanapalus on the verge of death is tentative about the precise nature of the 'lesson' this conflagration 'may' teach. His story, if rightly told, cannot be simple or clear-cut in the manner of epic or morality drama. This king leaves as his legacy to the future neither an empire, a self-justification, nor a straightforward confession of guilt. He leaves 'a problem'. The fire ensures only that this problem will be remembered: its interpretation and its application to the lives of later men, Sardanapalus (and Byron) refers to the intelligent consideration of an audience which may one day hammer out a better course of action through understanding the dilemmas of the past.

Byron's attitude towards the relationship of literature and life, objective and artistic truth, was even more tormented and ambiguous than that of the other Romantics.[10] Part of him was always impatient with poetry and its practitioners. As he grew older, however, he came to believe almost in spite of himself that

> words are things, and a small drop of ink,
> Falling like dew, upon a thought, produces
> That which makes thousands, perhaps millions, think.
>
> (*Don Juan*, III.lxxxviii)

This equivalence of words and things is stated again by Faliero just before his death: 'for true *words* are *things*' (v.i.289). Earlier in the tragedy the Doge's conviction that Time cares nothing for the intrinsic value of an action, but only for its failure or success, had clashed sharply with the idealism of Israel Bertuccio: 'They never fail who die / In a great cause' (II.ii.93–4). But Faliero modifies his stance at the end. He speaks 'to Time and to Eternity', and although the Forty have made sure that the Venetian people remain outside, 'beyond the compass of the human voice' (v.ii.24–6), that strange last scene of the play in which these anonymous citizens finally crowd onto the stage makes it plain that, although Faliero's actual words are inaudible, the watchers at the gate have somehow been able to extract a meaning from the sound. In the same spirit, Jacopo Foscari adds his name to the testimony accumulated on his prison wall and enjoins his wife to tell his story, and Sardanapalus heaps up his beacon-pyre.

Like Brecht, Byron aimed through his historical plays to change men's minds, to influence action. His Faliero, his Foscari, and his Sardanapalus are voices addressed to Greece under a tyranny, to the Italian patriots, to an England inching along towards the Reform Bill. As a dramatist, Byron is never didactic and doctrinaire, ungenerous in the way that Brecht is at his worst, but there are none the less some striking similarities in the way they approach the past. Both had a profound respect for the integrity of historical material. 'There are writers', Brecht once said in an interview, 'who simply set down what happened. I'm one of them. My material *is* intelligible; I don't first have to make it so.'[11] Byron felt this way about all of the historical subjects which attracted him. He would also have understood Brecht's passionate concern that the different social and political structures of past periods should be presented accurately on the stage: not in terms of farthingales, ruffs, or Assyrian costumes, but so that an audience should understand why men and women living under certain circumstances and conditions should have acted as they did.

Byron was not quite such a ferocious literary pirate as Brecht. He did not sit down to rewrite *Coriolanus*, or Marlowe's *Edward II*, or Farquhar's *The Recruiting Officer*, as Brecht unabashedly did. He did, however, create a continuity between his own plays and the great past of the English theatre. Byron used Shakespeare not as Keats and Shelley, Wordsworth or Charles Lamb used him, but in the way Shakespeare had used Marlowe, or Marlowe had built upon morality drama. In doing this he anticipated many of Brecht's attitudes and techniques. Byron too was concerned to minimise plot and the excessive importance of the ending, to regard each scene as an independent unit, to replace suggestion with argument, and honour reason over emotion for its own sake. Like Brecht, he wanted his audience to think, not to be transported out of itself into a world of day-dreams and somnambulist repose. He even understood about alienation. If the spectator is truly to confront himself and his own social reality through the medium of the stage, and to see what should be done to change it, he must not empathise with the actors. 'If I choose to see Richard III', Brecht argued, 'I don't want to feel myself to be Richard III, but to glimpse this phenomenon in all its strangeness and incomprehensibility.'[12] Hazlitt and Jeffrey criticised Byron for handling dramatic character in just this way.

Brecht discovered that he could not realise his dramatic aims without creating a special theatre in which his plays could be performed and training his own actors. Byron, who in any case had too many other occupations, would not and could not have done this. When *Marino Faliero*, predictably, failed at Drury Lane, he simply shrugged his shoulders and decided that from now on the text and not the play should be the thing. It may have been just as well. One remembers what happened when T. S. Eliot tried to revolutionise the London commercial theatre: that gradual deadening and flattening out of an original dramatic voice that had spoken out in *Sweeney Agonistes* and *Murder In The Cathedral*, as Eliot tried (with the well-intentioned assistance of E. Martin Browne) to succeed in the West End. Given his terror of failure, Byron might well have persuaded himself to take the easy and gratifying way out, and have written more plays like *Werner*. Instead, he moved on from the historical tragedies to *Cain, Heaven and Earth*, and that marvellous fragment, *The Deformed Transformed*. The modern experimental theatre has discovered these plays. For both Stanislavsky and Grotowski, a successful production of *Cain* proved to be a major step in their own artistic development. *The Deformed Transformed* was staged in London by Triple Action Theatre, playing at The Roundhouse, in 1972.[13] It would seem more than time that *Marino Faliero, The Two Foscari* and *Sardanapalus* should be staged, not as spectacles, but as plays to be understood, despite their use of the unities, in the light of the anti-Aristotelian, epic theatre of Brecht.

NOTES

1. Boleslaw Taborski, *Byron And The Theatre* (Salzburg Studies in English Literature, Salzburg, 1972) 229–56.
2. David Erdman, 'Byron's Stage-Fright', in *English Literary History*, VI (1939) 219–43.
3. Taborski, op. cit., 41.
4. Bertolt Brecht, 'A Short Organum For the Theatre', in *Brecht on Theatre*, trans. John Willett (London, 1964) 188.
5. William Hazlitt, from his unsigned review of *Marino Faliero, London Magazine* (May 1821). Quoted in *Byron: The Critical Heritage*, ed. Andrew Rutherford (London, 1970) 208–9.
6. Jeffrey, from unsigned reviews in the *Edinburgh Review* of September 1821 and April 1822. Quoted in Rutherford, op. cit., 210–11, 231–2.
7. Reginald Heber, from his unsigned review in the *Quarterly Review* (November 1822). Quoted in Rutherford, op. cit., 239.
8. Jerome McGann, in his otherwise admirable account of *The Two Foscari*, states that Loredano 'saves the council from public embarrassment by poisoning the Doge' (*Fiery Dust* (Chicago, 1968) 224). This is a misunderstanding of the last scene of the play, as the text itself – and Byron's own note on the subject of Foscari's death appended to *Marino Faliero* – make plain. (*Works,* ed. Page and Jump, 910)
9. Taborski, op. cit., 277.
10. Anne Barton, *Byron And the Mythology of Fact* (Nottingham Byron Lecture, 1968).
11. Brecht, quoted in *Brecht on Theatre*, 15.
12. Brecht, in *Brecht on Theatre*, 27.
13. Taborski, op. cit., 336–80.

9 ROMANCE IN BYRON'S *THE ISLAND**

P. D. Fleck

One of the principal impulses of romance is the fulfilment of dream or the portrayal of the world we want to live in as opposed to the one we do live in,[1] and one of the principal themes of Byron criticism is that the impulse did not work for Byron. We are familiar with this impulse of romance in such major romantic works as *The Prelude* and *Prometheus Unbound*. Wordsworth celebrates in his poem the preservation of the 'first/Poetic spirit of our human life' (II. 260–1) which spreads a 'sentiment of Being . . . O'er all that moves and all that seemeth still' (401–2) and creates an image of life 'All gratulant' (XIV. 387).[2] In the preface to *Prometheus Unbound*, Shelley describes the theme of his poem as 'beautiful idealisms of moral excellence'.[3] Neither Wordsworth nor Shelley is naively unaware of the great gulf fixed between the world we want and the world we have, and in the poetry of both there is a strong sense of the strain of bringing the two worlds into any kind of alignment, but there is also, overall, an equally strong sense of the possibility of doing so. In the preface to another of his poems, Shelley describes himself as one who 'without concealing the evil in the world is forever speculating how good may be made superior', and in the body of the poem itself he presents his faith in the possibility of the fulfilment of man's dreams in this way:

> See
> This lively child, blithe, innocent and free;
> She spends a happy time with little care,
> While we to such sick thoughts subjected are

* This chapter was originally presented as a lecture to the Byron Society.

> As came on you last night—it is our will
> That thus enchains us to permitted ill—
> We might be otherwise—we might be all
> We dream of happy, high, majestical.
> Where is the love, beauty, and truth we seek
> But in our mind? and if we were not weak
> Should we be less in deed than in desire?
>
> (166-76)

The poem is *Julian and Maddalo*, and Shelley is here addressing Byron, for in his eyes, as well perhaps as in our own, Byron tended to reject all possibility of the dream's fulfilment. 'You talk Utopia', Shelley has Byron reply, and later he has him remark that 'such aspiring theories' as Shelley himself espouses are 'vain' (201). The typical attitude of Byron in the presence of the romantic dream is one either of agonised awareness of its impossibility or of satiric detachment from the whole question.

But there is one poem in which Byron explores the romantic dream in quite a different way. It is *The Island*, the last complete poem he wrote. It is not a poem which has found the near universal praise accorded *Don Juan*, his last incomplete and probably incompletable work. Indeed, although recent critics, like R. F. Gleckner and J. J. McGann, to whom I am much indebted, have recognised its importance, others have called *The Island* 'a total failure' and a 'rag-bag of old Byronic themes'.[4] With these divergent views of the poem before me, I am mindful of the warning one Scott character gives another in *The Bride of Lammermoor*: 'sliddery ways crave wary walking'.[5] There are few poems of Byron more sliddery than *The Island*, and a wary walk through it will not reveal a totally new or different Byron from the one available to the careful reader of his better known poems. It will, however, reveal a Byron more sure-footed in the territory of romance than he has been given credit for. *The Island* is a remarkable experiment in which Byron departs from the most characteristic forms of his typical attitudes in a way that is at once unmistakably romantic and unmistakably Byronic.

The plot of the poem is deceptively simple. Closely following

William Bligh's own account,[6] Byron relates in the first canto the story of the mutiny on the *Bounty*. Longing for the tropical and lawless delights of Toobonai, the island paradise they had lingered on for six months, the mutineers, led by Fletcher Christian, take charge of the ship. They put the Captain and his followers afloat in a small craft and themselves set sail for the 'gentle' and 'genial' soil of the island. In the second canto, the delights of Toobonai are described with particular reference to the love of Torquil, a young mutineer from the Hebrides, and Neuha, a high-born native girl. Their idyll is interrupted at the end of the canto by the news that a British ship, which is almost certainly in search of the mutineers, has been sighted. Canto III begins after the main fight between the mutineers and the forces of justice has taken place and focuses upon their states of mind, with special emphasis upon the resigned melancholy of Christian. The canto concludes as Neuha arrives to bear them away from their enemies. In the final canto, one canoe takes Christian and two of his comrades to a high rock where they make their last stand, Christian, wounded and facing defeat, finally hurling himself upon the rocks below; the other canoe takes Torquil and Neuha to a secret subterranean cave which the lovers reach by diving into the ocean and appearing to drown and in which they hide until the forces of law and order have departed. At the end of the canto, they return to the island and live out 'such happy days/ As only the yet infant world displays' (IV. 419–20). The whole story is told with great gusto and, notwithstanding a number of apparent digressions, with a seldom slackening pace.

But apart from writing a rattling good yarn, Byron makes the whole design of the poem intricate and complex in ways that set *The Island* apart from his other tales. First of all, he juxtaposes the Byronic hero any reader of his earlier tales would expect to encounter with two others who are heroic in quite different ways. In the general sense, they are all heroes because Byron treats each of them sympathetically and gives each the centre of the stage at some point in the tale. In the more restrictive sense of the heroic as the quality that allows the chief character to rise while others fall, Bligh is the hero of the first canto, and Torquil of the rest of the poem; and Christian, the most Byronic of all three, is no hero at all. In order clearly to distinguish among them, I am going to reserve the term heroic for Bligh and use the terms tragic and romantic to describe the particular kind of heroism which applies to Christian and Torquil respectively. A second complexity of the poem, related to Byron's characterisation of these three figures, is that in dealing with each of the heroic, tragic, or romantic perspectives Byron adjusts his style. Another way of focusing on these adjustments is to say that the narrator of the story does not maintain an altogether synoptic or consistent view of the events he is relating but tends to adopt a view in keeping with the particular event of the moment. There are moments, too, when he adopts a comic style seemingly unrelated to any of the three perspectives already cited. In short, Byron has assembled those very perspectives and styles which he assembled in *Don Juan*, though he has here attempted to put their variety to quite a different use.

The principal characters of the poem are Bligh, Christian, Torquil, and Neuha. In romance, as Northrop Frye has pointed out, each character tends to be a 'stylized figure' expanding into 'a psychological archetype'.[7] The type in *The Island* whom we would expect to meet in a Byronic tale is Fletcher Christian. His dedication to his own freedom we have encountered in the heroes of Byron's early tales, and his awareness of the complexity of that freedom, in *Childe Harold, Manfred,* and *Cain*. He is unmistakably a 'Byronic hero': dark, brooding, melancholic, guilt-ridden, and alone. His character is asserted rather than demonstrated. Although we are told that 'Volumes lurked below' his cry in Canto I that he is 'in hell' (168, 164), we are given only glimpses into those volumes.[8] We are told that he is 'self-elected' to lead the mutiny (97), 'of a higher order' (III. 139), and 'stern and aloof' (III. 85). He feels keenly the 'sensation of his crime' (I. 98), and he feels acute responsibility for having involved others in it (III. 146). His determination to be 'fearless and free' (IV. 164) is a kind of 'madness' (IV. 146) and may have something to do with a past experience of love which the sight of Torquil and Neuha recalls to his mind. As he looks upon them reunited after the battle, his mood is one of 'gloomy joy'

> Mixed with those bitter thoughts the soul arrays
> In hopeless visions of our better days.
>
> (III. 204–6)

What those 'better days' were, we have no idea; and whether they were spent with an Astarte or a Medora, we do not know. What we do know is that he is incapable of commitment to anyone or anything, past or present, outside himself and the inevitability of his own tragic fate.

He tries to imagine that Torquil will be saved, but he cannot sustain that hope; and he takes up residence in sullen resignation and despair. In Canto IV, the despair mounts into a final expression of self which is at once tragic and absurd. From the outset, his attackers seem reluctant to do their work. They approach him and his comrades tentatively, calling for surrender and offering quarter; and when their tentativeness is answered with shrewdly aimed gunfire, they press vigorously up the slope, 'furious at the madness of their foes' (IV. 305). Even so, when, on the summit, they find Christian the sole survivor, barely alive and badly wounded, they offer mercy again. Christian revives to beckon to one of them to approach, and as he approaches, Christian loads his weapon with a vest button and smilingly shoots. Having allowed his self-absorption to mount to a last act of hatred for one who seeks to make some human contact with him, Christian, his 'wounded weary form . . . coiled . . . like a serpent', shakes his fist in defiant rage at the earth and hurls himself over the cliff, crushing his body on the rocks into 'one gory mass' which mixes with the weeds and bits of splintered weapon and is washed away by the ocean (336–50). Exit the Byronic hero. 'The rest was nothing, save a life misspent' (351). The increasing intensity with which Christian's last moments mount into his death and plummet with him into that word 'nothing', underscores the absurdity of Christian's stance. It is an absurdity we sense first in the detail of the vest button, which Byron assures us in a footnote with his customary fetish for fact, is drawn from real life, and we sense it also in the extravagance of Byron's description, which becomes almost a parody of his 'Corsair style'.[9] Almost a parody: here is our first 'sliddery way'. I said 'almost' because I think the approach to parody falls short of the humorous and the satiric and settles instead and finally into a pathetic and tragic rendering of the 'nothing' Christian has become. The absurd note is also struck in the incongruity of the flamboyant and extravagant prelude to a death that confirms the nothingness of his life, a nothingness, we are told in the closing lines of the passage, we have no business judging. Byron would appear to suspend side by side his own moral judgement of Christian, a judgement reinforced by his unequivocal view of Bligh, with his feeling for Christian's predicament and to effect the suspension in such a way that the judgement and the feeling do not interfere with each other, but are simply two facts which must be taken into account.

Bligh is perhaps the least complicated character in the poem, which is not to say he does not complicate it. If Christian is the tragic figure, Bligh is certainly the heroic. He is 'The Gallant Chief' (1.17). While most of his crew are dreaming of 'the cave/Of some soft savage' on Toobonai (1. 31–32), Bligh is dreaming of 'Old England's welcome shore' (19). England is his island, and he will overcome all obstacles to reach it, partly because he is in the right. Byron never questions his integrity nor his contention that he suffered at the hands of those whom he had treated well. But more than that, Bligh's dream will come true because he is determined that it should do so. He is unflinching and courageous in the event of the mutiny and at the prospect of the incredible suffering that he will have to endure in the perilous journey. The sketch Byron gives us of Bligh does not permit us to imagine that even in the depths of that journey we might ever hear him acknowledge that he was in hell. Discipline, self-control, and perseverance in fulfilling his dream are his virtues, and they stand in contrast to the lawlessness, the self-will, and the total despair of Christian. This contrast is a prelude to Byron's principal concern, which is the island and its dominant humour in Torquil and Neuha.

Torquil is a figure of romance in whom the potential for the tragic and the heroic coexist. He is a boy or a child. Indeed, more than Byron's Harold, Torquil is a *childe* in the romance sense of an aspirant and of one who evidences the potential for many things and the accomplishment of none. Raised in the Hebrides, he experienced 'the pensive moods' and 'the craggy solitudes' (II. 171–2) of a Fletcher Christian, but he shared them with the ocean with whom he identified himself completely (II. 167–74). 'The deep' was 'his home'. He might have been many things: a disciplined and humble soldier or a madman 'plunging for pleasure into pain' (187–93); an heroic or a tragic figure, in short, a Bligh or a Christian. He is neither here because, although he shares Christian's depth of spirit and his antipathy for the civilised world of law and order, he does not allow himself to be drowned in that depth; and although he shares Bligh's perseverance and self-control, he ultimately applies those virtues to a journey *through* the ocean to the island of love and not *on* the ocean to the island of law. In Canto II, he is 'A blooming boy, a truant mutineer' (209); in Canto IV, he becomes 'the Pilgrim of the Deep' (95).

The energy for life which this change from truant to pilgrim shapes in Torquil is intensified by an eager hope; or, as Byron puts it, in order to make the contrast with Christian explicit, Torquil is 'Acquainted with all feelings save despair' (II. 178). Even when Torquil's energy appears to wilt in Canto III, and we see him pale and weak, Byron is careful to insist 'that his faintness came not from despair' (97–103). The only major character in Byron with whom Torquil has any affinity in this regard is Don Juan. Like Juan, Torquil lives the life of immediacy and manages to recover from adversity in order to hurl himself into the next experience. But whereas Juan, as Alvin Kernan points out, 'is subjected to a criticism which deepens as the poem progresses',[10] the narrator of *The Island* has no criticism for Torquil and acknowledges only the potential of his destructiveness. He does not locate Torquil for us in the mutiny of Canto I any more than he locates Christian on the island of Canto II. He locates each in the natural habitat of his dominant characteristic, Torquil's being the hope and energy of life apparent in the island and Christian's being the despair and denial of life inherent in an act of mutiny. Torquil is a mutineer in the sense that all men are fallen creatures; Christian's rebelliousness, on the other hand, is a conscious and deliberate action, manifesting his dark and characteristic perversity.

Christian's affinity is with Satan; Torquil's with Adam. Satan and Adam are not in this poem, of course; Byron's is not here a vatic stance. But the analogy is helpful in understanding the difference between Christian and Torquil which is in the poem.

Torquil is not consumed with guilt because, like Don Juan, he becomes too much committed to present experience to be absorbed by the memory of himself in the last one. Many of Byron's heroes are plagued by the memory of some past 'dark delight' which prevents them from entering into the present moment.[11] Torquil yields to love and survives:

> No more the thundering memory of the fight
> Wrapped his weaned bosom in its dark delight;
> No more the irksome restlessness of Rest
> Disturbed him like the eagle in her nest,
> Whose whetted beak and far-pervading eye
> Darts for a victim over all the sky:
> His heart was tamed to that voluptuous state
> At once Elysian and effeminate . . .
>
> (II. 306–12)

The voluptuous and effeminate nature of Torquil's submission may suggest a kind of weak-kneed passivity, but we shall see that it is only one stage in his passage from truant to pilgrim and that the island and its life are much more than 'Elysian' and 'effeminate' suggest.

Before we turn to the island itself, however, we must examine the last of the poem's principal characters and the one most closely associated with the island's spirit. Neuha has been likened to Haidée and Dudù in *Don Juan*; but though there are likenesses, Neuha has none of the inherent predatoriness Bernard Blackstone has shown us in Haidée and none of the naiveté of Dudù.[12] Haidée is Nature's bride, Passion's child, and a lady of the cave;[13] Neuha is all of these and much more: she is a Naiad (II. 155), the nymph of the rivers and the streams, and a Nereid, the nymph of the Ocean (III. 184). She is as at home in the depths of the Ocean as she is on its surface, and she is as prepared to give herself up to it as she is to master it. In Canto II, she is still and calm and promises voluptuous rest (134); in Canto III, she leaps from her shell 'like a Nereid' (184) and snatches Torquil from death; she clears the breakers (226), and in Canto IV grapples with the sea, finally plunging into its depths to emerge its mistress.

> Such was this daughter of the southern seas,
> Herself a billow in her energies,
> To bear the bark of others' happiness,
> Nor feel a sorrow till their joy grew less:
> Her wild and warm yet faithful bosom knew
> No joy like what it gave.
>
> (II. 141–6)

Able to bear sorrow, willing to yield to the joy of others, suffused with an energy which makes despair as foreign to her nature as it is to Torquil's, Neuha is herself the spirit or the genius of the island.

She is also, of course, immensely shrewd and spunky. She is on the spot with canoes for escape when the mutineers are trapped, and she supervises the escape herself, ensuring that Christian and Torquil are separated. Nothing she does is fantastic or unexplained. A footnote assures us that her magic cave is real; and another, that its marvellous shapes have been encountered in a cave by a reliable witness. And there is to be no niggling, unanswered question as to the logistics of the cave's supplies. Anyone who has ever pondered the question: How, in *The Eve of St. Agnes*, did old Angela, infirm and doddery as she was, ever manage, inside what could have been no more than a few minutes, to haul up into Madeleine's room more 'cates and dainties' than one could eat in a day? need ponder no such question in Byron's romance. The magic cave in Canto IV is well-stocked for the romance feast, but the store of cocoa-nuts, yams, breadfruit, ripe bananas, sandal oil, fresh gnatoo, and other items, as unlike St Agnes' feast as Ben Bunting is unlike the Beadsman, were all in place, Byron is careful to tell us, because Neuha, in anticipation of the need, loaded her canoe 'Each dawn' (183) and 'Each eve' (185) and transported them there. If Neuha is more romantic a heroine than Haidée, she is, at the same time, as practical as Zoë. But the fullness of her character is not presented to us through satire and humour. In *Don Juan*, Haidée's adoration of Juan is accompanied by the sizzling sound of eggs frying (II. cxliv); in *The Island*, Neuha's love is accompanied by no such domestic music. But Byron lets us know, as it were, that she fries eggs.

To understand Neuha fully, we must understand the island of which she is the spirit; and here again romance is strengthened by a sense of reality. In the first canto, the *Bounty* is between two islands. One of them, England, is Bligh's, and though it is not described in any detail, we are told that it is characterised by discipline, duty, revenge, law, and fear and that Bligh will make a long and arduous return to it (177 ff.). The other is the Toobonai of the mutineers' imagination and is described in the simplest, Edenic terms: it is 'genial' and 'gentle' (107); its growth is gushing and its 'Plenty' is 'promiscuous' (35); its inhabitants are 'soft savages' (32), and they live in perpetual sun and summer (28). There is no 'lord' of the island; its only master is the 'mood' of those who live there (36–8). The terms Byron chooses to describe the island are deliberately designed to suggest a simple contrast between Nature and Civilisation, between the fulfilment and the curbing of desire. More than that, they suggest the soft immorality and voluptuous inactivity of Toobonai as contrasted with the nature of England, that other island to which Bligh is dedicated.

In Canto II, however, the perspective shifts from the mutineers' perception of the island to that of the islanders themselves. It is still a place of promiscuous plenty, but its geniality has not eliminated for those who live there the brute facts of death and of man's destructiveness. The song of the islanders with which the second canto opens outlines these facts in such a way as to give a double vision of both past and future. The past includes a time when the island was as Edenic as the mutineers remember it in Canto I; but that time is, for the islanders, only a 'memory bright' (II. 34), and now

> Forgotten is the rapture, or unknown,
> Of wandering with the Moon and Love alone.
>
> (38–9)

For the past also includes a time when the first 'shell of war' from Fiji descended upon the island and robbed it of its accustomed peace. The past, therefore, contains both the image of Eden and the image of its destruction. The future provides a similarly double focus. It includes not only the possibilities of either defeat or victory in the coming battle, but also the possibilities of a journey after death to the island of Bolotoo, the home of the Gods and of warriors who acquit themselves well in the battle, or of a journey into oblivion and nothingness.[14] The song attempts to subject these double images of past and future to the supremacy of the present moment, which is the supremacy of life itself. The present moment is one of joy in the beauty of the flowers on Toobonai's graves; and when the islanders wreathe themselves in those flowers, they obliterate neither the double facts of the past nor the double possibilities of the future; rather, they suspend themselves between them in the full intensity of the moment. The island does not, then, afford the total freedom imagined by the mutineers in Canto I; it cannot obliterate the past. But its natives have found a way of coping with the facts of 'death and all our woe' which for those who can embrace it, as Torquil can, affords a new and richer way of life.

It is a way like the way of art. The islanders' song is 'Tradition's ditty' (79), and it copes with the facts of history not by solidifying them into monuments and hieroglyphics for sages to labour over and students to dream in, but by yielding history to harmony so that labour and dream give way to an awakening of the heart (79–102). The harmony of the song, like that of art, is 'half divine' and 'leaves no record to the sceptic eye' (82–3); it holds in suspension a double vision. The song ends with the words:

> We too will see Licoo; but—oh! my heart!
> What do I say?—to-morrow we depart!
> (63–4)

Their passionate desire and their strong sense of reality are two facts of life which do not collide for the islanders, as they do for

Christian, and explode each other into nothingness. Instead, the two facts are rendered into song or art which awakens the heart to the power of the present moment. This is an important point, not only because it relates to the island as a place of possibility rather than the place of certain bliss the mutineers envisaged in the midst of their mutiny, but also because it relates to Byron's own technique in the poem as a whole of suspending or juxtaposing opposite views of the romantic dream.

The heart that is absorbed, like Christian's, in its own dark hell sleeps in a nightmare from which it cannot be awakened; but the heart, like Torquil's, that can yield itself up to another can be educated into an awakening. Torquil is a ready student, and Neuha, who, as we have seen, is the genius of the island, is a ready teacher. The idyllic love they share in Canto II is the fulfilment of all the longings that brought the mutineers back to the island, and there is nothing quite like it in the whole of Byron's work. It is here that we are most aware of the presence of Shelley. The lovers obliterate the past and the future (II. 353). They become caught in the tyranny of the present; they become caught in the tyranny of an ecstasy in which the spirit of each emerges from the self, recognises in the other a 'better self', and becomes one with that self, with the spirit of Nature, and with God. In Shelley's essay 'On Love', the soul is described as yearning for a better self 'deprived of all that we condemn or despise'. Such a self draws 'a circle around its proper paradise which pain and sorrow and evil dare not overleap'. The discovery of another in whom the soul's desire is fulfilled is, for Shelley, 'the invisible and unattainable point to which Love tends'.[15] The love of Torquil and Neuha reaches that point and describes a circle around them from which, to use Byron's phrases, 'Man's baseness' and 'Time's lesson' (II. 396) seem totally excluded. The terms of the attainment echo those Shelley employs in his *Epipsychidion*, another poem about two lovers who inhabit an island. Emily and her lover, in Shelley's poem, 'shall become the same . . . one/ Spirit within two frames . . .'

> One passion in twin-hearts, which grows and grew,
> Till like two meteors of expanding flame,

> Those spheres instinct with it become the same,
> Touch, mingle, are transfigured; ever still
> Burning, yet ever inconsumable.
>
> (573–9)

In Byron's poem, Torquil and Neuha find in each other

> The other better self, whose joy or woe
> Is more than ours; the all-absorbing flame
> Which, kindled by another, grows the same,
> Wrapt in one blaze; the pure, yet funeral pile,
> Where gentle hearts, like Bramins, sit and smile.
>
> (377–81)

The self finds its identity not only in the better self of the loved one but also in the spirit of Nature, so that for the lover 'All Nature is his realm, and Love his throne' (397).

Shelley, too, makes this point in his essay and in his poem, but in the lines which celebrate Nature's 'reply . . . to our intelligence' in the second canto of *The Island* (382–97), it is the Wordsworthian echo that resounds most clearly. Indeed, there is no poem of Byron that manifests more strikingly the acceptance of two concepts that we usually associate with Wordsworth. The ideas that 'Nature never did betray/The heart that loved her' and that 'The Child is Father of the Man'[16] are firmly planted in Byron's insistence that 'Nature's native scenes' are

> Loved to the last, whatever intervenes
> Between us and our Childhood's sympathy,
> Which still reverts to what first caught the eye.
> He who first met the Highlands' swelling blue
> Will love each peak that shows a kindred hue,
> Hail in each crag a friend's familiar face,
> And clasp the mountain in his Mind's embrace.
>
> (II. 276–83)

These lines follow those which describe Torquil and Neuha as 'children of the isles' (274) and expand on Byron's earlier association of Torquil's eagerness of hope and total abstinence from despair with his childhood on the wild and beautiful Hebrides island, surrounded by an ocean which he made his 'home'. Byron does indeed change Wordsworth's lakes for ocean, but the change is to the form of Wordsworth's claims for Nature and not to their substance. 'Fostered alike by beauty and by fear', Torquil's soul had what Wordsworth calls in *The Prelude* 'Fair seed-time' (302, 301) and grew to know that the spirit which informs Nature has to take up firm residence in the self. Only then can it cope with what he calls in 'Tintern Abbey' the 'evil tongues, /Rash judgments' and 'sneers of selfish men' and 'the dreary intercourse of daily life' (129–31). In *The Island* the dreariness and the evil are 'Time's lesson' and 'Man's baseness' (396), and it is in the moments of love and the moments of communion with the spirit of Nature that these forces are overcome. They are not obliterated, except temporarily in the first heady ecstasy of love, but they *are* overcome: as Wordsworth makes clear in 'Tintern Abbey', though 'the burthen of the mystery' is 'lightened' (38–41), the mystery remains, and, as Shelley argues in his essay, love tends toward a point which is unattainable. My purpose in attempting to illuminate Byron's theme by alluding to Shelley and Wordsworth is not to suggest that he had them specifically in mind, though that is certainly possible and much more needs to be done on the influence of both poets upon Byron's work; my purpose, rather, is to illustrate by analogy how centrally Romantic are Byron's concerns in this poem and how those concerns are expressed in terms which he shared with his contemporaries but used in his own way.

The first stage of Torquil's education is the experience of love in his union with Neuha, and that experience radiates from the 'one blaze' of their love, outward encompassing 'All Nature'. The second stage is the intrusion of 'Man's baseness' and 'Time's lesson' upon that love. The intrusion of 'Time's lesson' is suggested in the setting of the sun, which

> Plunged with red forehead down along the wave,
> As dives a hero headlong to his grave.
>   (364–5)

These lines not only announce dramatically a threat to Torquil and Neuha; they also foreshadow the symbolic plunge into the ocean the 'one blaze' of their love must undergo, into a funeral cave from which they will emerge newborn, as will the sun from the ocean.[17] For the present, the lovers merely wonder 'that Summer showed so brief a sun', and ask 'if indeed the day were done?' (368–9). The answer comes in the form of a 'loud, long, and naval whistle' (428), accompanied by the hoarse cries of Ben Bunting, breaking the peace of the sunless night and announcing the intrusion of 'Man's baseness'. But before we let Ben have his say, there are a few more landmarks we should briefly observe from the sliddery heights of romance.

Ben's cries summon Torquil to begin a perilous journey which takes him from his Edenic island through a wasteland where he will be tested, where he will die a symbolic death, and where he will be born again. His journey across the sullen ocean to 'A black rock' (IV. 10), the faith in Neuha which prompts him to dive after her into the ocean as to his death, and the consummation of the lovers in the womb-like cave and their subsequent rising from the cave and the sea, all repeat the essential plot of romance. There had been a consummation in Canto II, but it had abstracted the lovers from the dark realities of life. The Torquil who is born again in Canto IV springs from the union in the cave of both dark and bright realities. The cave is a 'Chapel of the Seas', symbolising in its 'central realm of earth' (119), in its 'darkness' alleviated only by 'a sobered ray' of daylight (131–2), in the 'fantastic faces' which 'moped and mowed on high' (156) and in its shapes of 'mitre', 'shrine', and 'seeming crucifix', something of the reality from which the lovers had abstracted themselves in the 'blaze' of their love in Canto II. But this dark shadowy reality is lightened by the laughter (118), the joy (128), and the smiles of Neuha (187), and by her own spirit which makes the 'subterranean world serene' (178). She has brought the golden fruit and joy of the island into the dark world and made it light and rich. Torquil's journey has brought him to his shrine. No longer a mere 'truant', he has become a 'Pilgrim of the Deep' (IV. 95).

The legend of the cave that Neuha tells is as important for an understanding of the island as the song of the islanders in Canto II. It is a legend which tells of triumph over 'a desperate feud' by a symbolic death which becomes a rebirth into a new and happier life; and it reaffirms that the island, whatever its first appearance and whatever the first experience of it, is a place whose spirit, though it cannot and does not exclude 'Man's baseness' and 'Time's lesson', can overcome them through a rendering up of self in love. After the rest of the mutineers have been rounded up, the ocean heaves for them 'calm and careless', 'Eternal with unsympathetic flow' (IV. 367–8); as epitomised in Christian, they have been unable to yield themselves to the island's spirit and are now ironically either the prisoners of law or of death. For Torquil and Neuha, that same ocean is 'Joy' (387), and they return to 'Peace and Pleasure, perilously earned', to enjoy

> A night succeeded by such happy days
> As only the yet infant world displays.
>
> (418–20)

The island is the state of mind which makes their return possible.

I have been suggesting that most of the poem is devoted to the romantic treatment of Torquil and Neuha and that they and the island form the centre of its principal concern, but there are, of course, pressures from the periphery. Bligh is one of them; he disappears from the poem at the end of Canto I as he sets out on a voyage as horrendous as the Ancient Mariner's, but what he represents never entirely departs from the poem and is a part of the full meaning of the 'yet' in the last lines. More of that in a moment. Ben Bunting's hoarse cries must now be heard, for his appearance at the end of Canto II is the most frequently observed pressure upon the romance of the poem. After the full and fiery rendering of love which settles into a hush of peace and piety, in rushes Ben, blowing loud whistles, shouting, and reeking of tobacco. The obvious point is that the lovers have been lulled into obliterating the past and the future, and that is a state of mind which cannot be permanent. Just as the islanders have to test the validity of their life against the harsh reality of the Fiji warriors and come out of their simple Eden, so the lovers have to encounter the reality of 'death and all our woe' and the British navy. But there is more to Ben's arrival than that. The effect Byron achieves is to make the romance of the lovers look real as compared to the ridiculousness of Ben. The paean to tobacco as a soporific and a drug (448–59) stands in contrast to the charm and spell of love. It is Ben, and not Torquil and Neuha, who is 'fantastic' (462) on the island; it is he, and not they, who is engaged in a 'savage masquerade' (463); and it is he, and not they, who is untouched by the island and cannot come out of himself. Portsmouth, the Pole, Stamboul, Wapping or the Strand – they are all the same to Ben. He wanders the earth without ever becoming a part of it, but Torquil and Neuha become one with all of Nature.

Ben is the comic version of Christian. He can no more strip himself of his identity than Christian can. The ceremony of crossing the line in which the god appears to rise from the sea born anew (463–73) is a burlesque of the rising of the lovers from the sea in Canto IV. And whereas the island has already initiated Torquil into love, and the ritual of Canto IV will initiate him into a new life, Ben is initiated into no more than a weird 'garb' which his 'former state' irrepressibly dominates. Byron's final word for this 'garb' is 'heteroclite' (499), and Paul West takes the view that this word does some 'exquisite wrecking'.[18] But I am not sure that 'wrecking' is the right term. 'Heteroclite' means eccentric, irregular, and anomalous, and that is precisely what Ben is in this setting. The word does not wreck Ben so much as it describes him. Nor does he wreck Torquil and Neuha, though he may seem to come close to doing so. At the very end of the canto, Torquil professes an undying love for Neuha which amuses Ben:

> 'But whatsoe'er betide, ah, Neuha! now
> Unman me not: the hour will not allow
> A tear; I am thine whatever intervenes!'
> 'Right,' quoth Ben; 'that will do for the marines.'
>
> (528–31)

To the wildly romantic protestations of Torquil and the worldly scepticism of Ben, Byron adds this matter-of-fact footnote:

> 'That will do for the marines, but the sailors won't believe it,' is an old saying: and one of the few fragments of former jealousies which still survive (in jest only) between these gallant services.

I take the function of the note not merely to let us in on the jest if we should happen to have missed it but also perhaps to let us know that in the poem it *is* a jest and not an explosive device. It allows us to retreat from the intensity of the romance without retreating from its substance.

Ben is wrecked, of course, in Canto IV, though without the attention given Christian, so that by the end of the poem what is left in suspension is the infant world of Torquil and the mature world of Bligh, the world we want and the world we must make our way in. The first and fourth cantos end as Bligh and Torquil each set out in a slender bark for a different island. In the intervening cantos, the central values of Bligh and his island are not eradicated from the poem's concern, but they are pushed to the periphery where they remind us not of a certainty which intrudes upon the possibility of love on Toobonai but of another possibility altogether. In the end, Byron accepts both. And why not? He had made clear enough in his reactions to the critics of *Don Juan* that he meant in that poem to portray life itself, by allowing moments of romantic and tragic intensity to jostle freely and frequently with moments of scepticism and satire.[19] In *The Island*, the humour is more restrained and gives way to a seriousness which is neither solemn nor satiric, a seriousness, Byron suggests in his headnote to the poem, based partly upon the fact of the mutiny and partly on the fact of the island, and a seriousness, he suggests to Leigh Hunt, which will interweave what unenlightened readers will think of as 'pamby' with what Byron intends as '*un*common-place'.[20] The suspension of the two possibilities is best exemplified in the song of the islanders, with its equal emphasis upon 'We will see Licoo' and 'tomorrow we depart', suggesting that the island itself is a place where both statements are valid. The darker possibility does not disappear from the poem, but by Canto IV it has assumed a place on the borders of Torquil's experience, not unlike the place of Jupiter at the foot of Demogorgon's throne on the outer periphery of the rejoicing at the end of *Prometheus Unbound*.[21] That Shelley's work is a lyrical drama and Byron's is a tale should not prevent us from acknowledging that what is unmistakably romantic in *The Island* is the acceptance of the possibility of the dream's fulfilment. What is unmistakably Byronic is the presence of the seemingly disparate elements with which that possibility is presented. And what leads one to see in *The Island* a remarkable experiment is the quite different service to which the elements are put, a service which they were not to perform again in the cantos of *Don Juan* Byron wrote in the last year of his life. Those cantos deal with the centrality of Bligh's island, and the possibility of a civilised Toobonai is there located on an outer sphere where the mysterious figure of Aurora Raby shimmers and waits. Whether the romantic possibility could have found a place in the centre again is a matter for speculation. Perhaps the way of *The Island* would have proved too sliddery after all.

NOTES

1 Northrop Frye, *The Anatomy of Criticism* (Princeton, 1957) 106, 162 and *passim*. See also Frye, *Fearful Symmetry* (Princeton, 1947) 26.
2 *The Poetical Works of William Wordsworth*, ed. Thomas Hutchinson (Oxford, 1956) 505, 507, 588. All quotations from Wordsworth's poems are from this edition.
3 *The Poems of Shelley*, ed. Thomas Hutchinson (Oxford, 1960) 207. All quotations from Shelley's poems are from this edition.
4 R. F. Gleckner, *Byron and the Ruins of Paradise* (Baltimore, 1967) 347–50; and J. J. McGann, *Fiery Dust: Byron's Poetic Development* (Chicago, 1968) 186–202. For 'a total failure', see John A. Symonds, quoted in *Byron: The Critical Heritage*, ed. A. Rutherford (London, 1970) 413; and for 'rag-bag of old Byronic

themes', see A. Rutherford, *Byron: A Critical Study* (Stanford, 1962) 202.
5 *Everyman* edition (London, 1973) 97.
6 William Bligh, *A Narrative of the Mutiny on Board His Majesty's Ship Bounty* . . . (London, 1790).
7 *The Anatomy of Criticism* (Princeton, 1957) 196.
8 All references to the poem are from *The Works of Lord Byron: Poetry*, ed. E. H. Coleridge (London, 1901) v 587–639.
9 Byron told Leigh Hunt (25 January 1823) that he wanted to avoid 'running foul of [his] own *Corsair* and style, so as to produce repetition and monotony' (*The Works of Lord Byron: Letters and Journals*, ed. R. E. Prothero (London, 1901) VI 164–5).
10 *The Plot of Satire* (New Haven, 1965) 201–2.
11 Cf. *Lara* and *Manfred*, for a start.
12 *The Lost Travellers* (London, 1962) 201–2. Blackstone sees 'an ambivalence' in Neuha (p. 195), but he does not see it as constituting as fundamental a quality of character as the ambivalence of Haidée.
13 *Don Juan*, II. ccii, cxx.
14 Byron does not make the nature of Bolotoo explicit in his poem, but the reference makes clear that it is a place associated with the Gods. For an account of Bolotoo, see Byron's source: John Martin, *Mariner's Account of the Tonga Islands* (London, 1817) II, Chap. v.
15 'Essay on Love' in *Shelley's Prose: or The Trumpet of a Prophecy*, ed. David L. Clark (Albuquerque, New Mexico, 1966) 170.
16 'Tintern Abbey', ll. 122–3; epigraph to the 'Intimations Ode'.
17 See also the image in ll 137–40, where Neuha's beauty is compared to the coral which 'draws the diver to the crimson cave'.
18 *Byron and the Spoiler's Art* (London, 1960) 95.
19 See especially the letter to Murray (12 August 1819), *Letters and Journals*, IV 339–46, in which Byron answers the objection of a critic 'to the quick succession of fun and gravity' (341). Byron argues that in *Don Juan* 'the gravity . . . (in intention at least) heighten[s] the fun'; I would argue that the 'fun' heightens the 'gravity' in *The Island*. For a full account of Byron's arguments on this point as it relates to *Don Juan*, see T. G. Steffan, *Byron's*

Don Juan, 1: *The Making of a Masterpiece* (Austin, Texas, 1957) 3–60.

20 See the letter to Leigh Hunt cited in note 9. I disagree with Andrew Rutherford's view that Byron in this letter makes clear that he 'thought very little of this poem' (Rutherford, 202). In the first place, Byron was quite frequently tentative about his work before it was published (the history of his view of *Don Juan* is a case in point); secondly, Leigh Hunt seems a somewhat unlikely correspondent for the degree of self-criticism Rutherford attaches to the letter; and thirdly, Rutherford seems to miss the whole of what Byron is saying: . . . 'the most pamby portions of the Toobonai Islanders will be the most agreeable to the enlightened public, *though I shall sprinkle some uncommonplace here and there nevertheless.*—"*Nous verrons.*"' [Italics mine]. The force and context of 'enlightened' is 'unenlightened', and Byron's sprinklings include, I think, both the Ben Bunting episode and the realistic view of the island taken by the islanders themselves. Byron's letter suggests that portions of the poem taken out of context will seem very 'pamby' indeed but that the context itself will include the '*un*common-place' in a romance poem. The problem of the experiment is clear in his mind, but the outcome is not. The message in '"*Nous verrons*"' is less that Byron 'thought very little' of *The Island* than that he may have hoped for much.

21 Cf. McGann, *Fiery Dust* (201–2): 'As an allegory, then, *The Island* should probably be regarded as normative rather than definitive. It describes the term of man's furthest hopes but does not offer – any more than *Prometheus Unbound* does – the picture of a necessary personal or political future. Both poems are prophecies in the basic sense: they delineate a form of human possibility which yet requires the choice that determines accomplishment, a choice, moreover, that must be reaffirmed constantly. The vision of *The Island* is true because it may be true, always.'

INDEX

(References contained in notes have not been indexed.)

Address, . . . at . . . Drury-Lane Theatre, 140
Aeschylus, 153
Alexander I, Tsar, 30, 72
Alfieri, Vittorio, 140
Arnold, Matthew, 37, 42, 47, 51, 58–9, 66
Auden, W. H., 37, 39, 45
Austen, Jane, 9, 49–50, 120, 128, 133

Bar, Francis, 107
Barton, Anne, xiii, xv, 138–62
Beckett, Samuel, 75
Beppo, x, xii, 39, 52, 58, 91–2, 113, 119, 125, 127
Berry, Francis, ix, xi, xv, 35–51
Bettesworth, George E. B., 2
Bettesworth, J. T. P., 12
Bible, 132
Blackstone, Bernard, 170
Blackwood's Magazine, 126
Bland, Robert, 19–22
Bligh, William, 165
Blücher, Marshal, 30
Bonaparte, Napoleon, 29–30, 45, 60, 71, 72, 141
Boscawen, Fanny, 2, 4
Bottrall, Ronald, 94
Bradley, F. H., 40
Brecht, B., xiii, 142, 151, 156, 160–2
Bride of Abydos, The, 49
Browne, E. Martin, 161
Brydges, Sir Egerton, 83–4
Burney, Fanny, 2, 4, 5–6
Butler, Samuel (author of *Hudibras*), 100–1
Byron, Allegra (the poet's daughter), 27
Byron, Lady Annabella (the poet's wife), 7, 8, 10, 13–14, 45, 60, 139, 148
Byron, Augusta, *see* Leigh, Mrs Augusta
Byron, Augusta Ada (the poet's daughter), 13, 14
Byron, Mrs Catherine Gordon, viii, 1, 6
Byron, John (the poet's father), 1, 3, 5, 6
Byron, Admiral John, viii, 1–3, 5, 6
Byron, Julia, 10
Byron, Mrs Sophia, *see* Trevanion, Sophia
Byronic hero, ix, x, xi, 46–7, 54, 71–5, 84, 165–8, 169–70

C., Susan, 20–1
Cain, 26–8, 68, 138, 139, 155, 161, 166
Castlereagh, Viscount Robert Stewart, 59
Cervantes Saavedra, M. de, 156
Charlotte, Queen, 8
Chester Cycle, The, 155
Childe Harold's Pilgrimage, ix, x, 41–51, 54, 55, 58, 60, 62, 63, 64–5, 70–5, 79, 84, 85–6, 87–90, 91, 92, 114, 116–18, 119, 120, 121, 122, 123, 126, 138, 166, 168
Churchill, Charles, 92
Clare, John, 48–9

185

Index

Coleridge, S. T., 42, 54, 56, 79, 81, 121, 140, 151–2, 178
Corsair, The, 7, 89, 167
Cowper, William, 92
Curse of Minerva, The, 116

Dallas, R. C., 82
Darkness, 68
Deformed Transformed, The, 161
Della Cruscans, 78
Dennis, John, 76, 120
Destruction of Sennacherib, The, 68–9
Don Juan, x, xi, xii, xiii, 3, 22–3, 26, 37, 39, 51, 52, 53, 59–60, 61, 68, 74, 75, 78, 94–111, 113, 119, 121, 122, 123, 125, 126, 127, 128–31, 133–7, 138, 159, 164, 166, 169, 170–2, 180, 181
Dostoyevsky, F. M., 73
Dryden, John, 39, 41, 56, 77, 78, 121, 127

Eckermann, J. P., 35
Edinburgh Review, 60, 77, 79, 117, 118, 143
Elgin, Lord, 116
Eliot, George, 37
Eliot, T. S., ix, 9, 36–40, 45, 47, 50, 75, 94, 161
England, A. B., xi, xii, xv, 94–112
English Bards, and Scotch Reviewers, 55, 77, 78–82, 90–1, 118–19, 121, 132
Erdman, David, 139

Farquhar, George, 160
Fielding, Henry, 130–1, 135
Fleck, P. D., xiii, xv, 163–83
Fletcher, William, 89, 115, 123
Foot, Michael, viii
Ford, John, 153
Frere, J. H., xii, xiii, 91, 125
Frye, Northrop, 166
Fussell, Paul, 98

Garrick, David, 140

Gautier, Théophile, x
George III, King, 59, 131, 132
Giaour, The, ix–x, 49–50, 65–6, 75
Gibbon, Edward, 9, 55
Gifford, William, xii, 78–80, 117, 120, 138
Gleckner, R. F., 67, 74, 164
Goethe, J. W. von, x, 35–7, 39, 46–7, 52, 60, 68
Goldsmith, Oliver, 18, 121
Gray, May, 67
Gray, Thomas, 36–7
Grotowski, Jerzy, 161
Guiccioli, Count Alessandro, 29
Guiccioli, Countess Teresa, 29, 51

Harness, William, 21–2, 25–6
Hazlitt, William, 142–3, 146, 161
Heaven and Earth, 155, 161
Heber, Reginald, 143
Hebrew Melodies, 68–9
Heine, Heinrich, x
Hints from Horace, 77, 91, 116–18, 119–20
Hobhouse, John Cam, 18–21, 25, 29, 115, 123
Hodgson, Francis, 20–2, 122, 126
Holland, Lady Elizabeth, 32
Holland, Lord, 24, 32
Homer, 117
Horace, 76, 92, 115, 116, 121
Hours of Idleness, 77, 117, 118
Hugo, Victor, x
Hunt, Leigh, 180

Irving, Henry, 139
Island, The, xiii, 164–83

James, Henry, 40
Jeffrey, Francis, 49, 52, 60, 77, 81–2, 85, 117, 143, 161
Jeffries [Jeffreys], Judge, 81–2
Johnson, Samuel, 2, 4–5, 55, 78, 89–90, 131

Jonson, Ben, 155
Joseph, M. K., 67–8, 70
Joyce, James, 74–5
Juvenal, 76, 77, 88, 90, 121, 127

Kant, Immanuel, 84–5
Kean, Edmund, 140, 141, 143, 146
Keats, John, 37, 41–2, 43, 54, 56–7, 59, 140, 151–2, 160, 171
Kernan, Alvin, 169
Kinnaird, Douglas, 29
Kipling, Rudyard, 38
Knight, G. Wilson, 16, 39, 42, 151

Lamartine, A. de, x, 74
Lamb, Charles, 160
Lament of Tasso, The, 49
Landon, Letitia E., 10
Lara, 86–7, 88
Lawrence, D. H., 62
Leavis, F. R., 94
Lee, Nathaniel, 153
Leigh, Mrs Augusta, viii, 3–4, 7, 8, 10–11, 12, 13, 14, 25, 29, 32, 58
Leigh, George, 4, 8, 11
Leigh, Georgiana, 4, 8, 10, 11, 13, 14
Leigh, Medora, viii, 4, 7–8, 10–14
Leopardi, Giacomo, x
Lermontov, M. Y., x, 72–3
Lines to Mr Hodgson, 122–3, 126
Lockhart, J. G., 126

MacNeice, Louis, 39
Macready, W. C., 139, 156
Manfred, x, 67–8, 114, 138, 155, 166, 167
Marchand, L. A., xiv, 16n, 17, 55, 65
Marino Faliero, xiii, 139, 142–52, 154, 155, 159–60, 161
Marlowe, Christopher, 155, 156, 160
Massinger, Philip, 140
Mazeppa, 66
McGann, J. J., 164
Melbourne, Lady Elizabeth, 26

Milbanke, Annabella, *see* Byron, Lady
Milbanke, Lady Judith, 89
Milbanke, Sir Ralph, 23
Mille, Cecil B. de, 142
Milton, John, 68, 128, 132
Molière, 128
Montagu, Mrs Elizabeth, 2, 4
Moore, Thomas, xiii, 16–17, 23, 25, 26–8, 29, 58, 82, 85, 118, 123–6, 138
Mozart, Wolfgang Amadeus, 128
Murray, John, 25, 26, 28, 29, 55, 58, 59, 60, 62, 90, 91, 92, 124, 126, 138, 139, 141, 143, 144, 145, 146, 155, 156
Musset, Alfred de, x
Mussolini, Benito, 40

Nash, John, 1, 10, 12
Nelson, Viscount Horatio, 2

O Hehir, Brendan, 108
O'Higgins, Mr, 33–4
Ottava rima, xiii, 39, 43, 51, 60, 91, 126, 127, 129
Otway, Thomas, 144, 145, 148
Ovid, 127–8

Peacock, T. L., 130
Peele, George, 155
Phelps, Gilbert, x–xi, xii, xiii, xvi, 52–75
Phelps, Samuel, 139
Pinter, Harold, 75
Piozzi, Gabriel, 4–5
Piozzi, Mrs Hester, *see* Thrale, Mrs Hester
Pope, Alexander, xii, xiii, 39, 41, 42, 54–6, 57, 59, 62, 64, 77, 78–81, 83, 90, 94–100, 101, 105, 108, 111, 116–35 *passim*
Pordage, Samuel, 155
Prince Regent (later King George IV), 123
Prisoner of Chillon, The, 49, 65, 68, 114

Prometheus, 67
Prothero, R. E., xiv, 16n, 17
Pulci, Luigi, 91, 125
Pushkin, Alexander, x, 72

Racine, Jean, 152
Read, Herbert, 37–8, 56
Robson, W. W., 56
Rochester, John Wilmot (Earl of), 56
Rommel, E., 155
Rossini, G. A., 128
Rowlandson, Thomas, 122
Rowse, A. L., viii, xvi, 1–15
Ruddick, W., xi, xii–xiii, xvi, 113–37
Ruffhead, Owen, 54
Rutherford, Andrew, 164

Sand, George, x
Sardanapalus, xiii, 138, 139, 142, 144, 155–9, 160, 161
Schwarzenberg, Prince Karl Philipp, 30
Scott, Sir Walter, 49–50, 52, 63, 68, 79, 121, 128, 164, 167
Scrutiny, 37
Segati, Marianna, 25
Shakespeare, William, 1, 82, 140, 141, 144–5, 148, 150, 151–2, 153, 154, 155, 156, 160
Shelley, P. B., 43, 52, 68, 140, 160, 163, 174–6, 181
Sheridan, R. B., 141, 153, 155
Siddons, Mrs Sarah, 140
Siege of Corinth, The, 78
Sligo, Marquis of, 115
Smollett, Tobias, 122, 131
Solzhenitsyn, Alexander, 152–3
Southey, Robert, 59, 79, 81, 82, 118, 131–2
Spenser, Edmund, 42–3, 127–8
Spenserian stanza, 42–3, 63, 64
Stanislavsky, K. S. 161
Sterne, Laurence, 121, 135
Storey, David, 75

Swift, Jonathan, xii, 54, 77, 85, 87, 100–11, 135
Swinburne, A. C., 52, 61
Symonds, John Addington, 57, 61, 164

Tennyson, Alfred, 14
Thackeray, W. M., 131
Theobald, Lewis, 77
There Be None of Beauty's Daughters, 56
Thomson, James, 42
Thrale, Mrs Hester, 2–7
Trevanion, Ada, 14
Trevanion, Henry, viii, 4, 8–14
Trevanion, John, 10
Trevanion, Marie Violette, 13
Trevanion, Sophia, viii, 1–7
Two Foscari, The, xiii, 36, 47, 138, 139, 142, 144, 151–5, 160, 161
Turney, Catherine, 8

Vigny, Alfred de, x
Virgil, 107
Vision of Judgment, The, x, xiii, 52, 113, 131–3
Voltaire, 5

Wakefield Master, The, 155
Waltz, The, 90–1, 120, 136
Webster, James Wedderburn and Lady Frances, 26
Wellington, Arthur Wellesley (Duke of), 59
Werner, 138–9, 141, 142, 161
West, Paul, 64, 179
Wild Gazelle, The, 68–9
Wordsworth, William, 40, 41–2, 54, 55, 56, 59, 62, 72, 79, 81, 118, 121, 140, 160, 163, 175–6
World, 79

Yarker, Patrick, xi–xii, xiii, xvi, 76–93
Yeats, W. B., x, 40, 50, 75
York Cycle, The, 155